Trading Composure

Trading Composure

Mastering Your Mind for Trading Success

Yvan Byeajee

WILEY

Published by John Wiley & Sons, Inc., Hoboken, New Jersey.
Published simultaneously in Canada.

For general information on our other products and services or for technical support,
please contact our Customer Care Department within the United States at (800) 762-
2974, outside the United States at (317) 572-3993 or fax (317) 572-4002.

Wiley also publishes its books in a variety of electronic formats. Some content that
appears in print may not be available in electronic formats. For more information
about Wiley products, visit our web site at www.wiley.com.

Library of Congress Cataloging-in-Publication Data is available:

ISBN 9781394244447 (cloth)
ISBN 9781394244461 (epub)
ISBN 9781394244454 (epdf)

Cover Design: Wiley
Cover Image: © M-image/iStock /Getty Images
Author Photo: Courtesy of the Author
SKY10079834_072224

To the remarkable students of the Consistent Trader Program: I dedicate this book to you. Your experiences affirm that the correct mindset for trading isn't just innate but can be transmitted, cultivated, and sustained. Thank you for being the shining examples of what it means to embrace and live out the principles shared in this book.

Contents

Preface

Composure
noun

The ability to remain serene and collected, particularly amidst adversity.
Similar: equanimity, self-control, level-headedness

Imagine a tranquil lake, its surface like a flawless mirror reflecting the expansive sky and surrounding forest. Even when stirred by winds, causing ripples to dance across its surface, the lake's depths remain quiet and undisturbed. The state of composure, much like the depth of that lake, embodies a state of profound inner peace and equilibrium. It's not merely about appearing calm on the surface but having an inner reservoir of stillness that isn't easily disrupted by the storms of life—or the market, in the case of trading.

In 2006, when I transitioned from the security of a regular paycheck to the exhilarating yet turbulent world of financial markets, I underestimated the pivotal role that composure plays in achieving trading success. Like many, I thought that mastery of chart analysis was the sole requirement for success in this endeavor. Operating from a mindset entirely focused on prediction, the allure of quick riches overshadowed all else. I believed that with just the right tools and strategies, I could conquer every swell and ebb of the market.

But if predicting the market is as straightforward as it seems, one might wonder why our cities aren't teeming with newly minted billionaires. Why aren't Lamborghinis lining our streets? Moreover, why do statistics consistently reveal that most traders lose more than they make (Rolf 2019)? These piercing questions never crossed my mind back then, being too blinded by the lure of vast riches. However, as the months rolled by, the reality of trading started to sink in. It became abundantly clear that charts, tools, and strategies were merely instruments in an orchestra. And like any orchestra, success wasn't just about playing each instrument flawlessly but about harmonizing them with the one element I had overlooked: my mindset.

From a young age, I knew that I was going to have a life as a risk manager. This conviction stemmed from an innate pull to understand and control the uncertainties of my life. I was raised in a broken family—divorced parents, a mother battling psychological demons, the constant specter of financial strain—and chaos indelibly etched its mark on my worldview; it became the crucible in which unproductive beliefs and patterns took root, shaping my experiences of life. Then, during my teenage years, I discovered trading, and it ignited an immediate passion and sense of purpose within me. At the time, I couldn't quite pinpoint why I was so mesmerized by the intricate world of financial markets. On the surface, it seemed to be all about the money. After all, in trading, fortunes can be made in the blink of an eye. However, with time, I've come to realize that my fascination ran much deeper than mere financial gain. It wasn't just about the potential for wealth; it was about something far more profound. It was about my innate yearning to conquer uncertainty and chaos, as those were recurring themes in my life.

Needless to say, one doesn't just "conquer chaos." If it were as simple as that, the landscape of successful traders would be vastly different. At this juncture, success would simply hinge on crunching numbers, pinpointing chart patterns and formations, executing trades, and immediately enjoying the rewards. However, reality paints a more nuanced picture. Market dynamics are imbued with an inherent uncertainty that defies analysis and prediction. Most people don't want to hear this harsh reality—they prefer the allure of quick fixes and guaranteed profits. Nevertheless, confronting the truth of uncertainty head-on is essential for anyone seeking long-term success in trading.

While it may initially appear that the presence of uncertainty casts trading pursuits in a negative light, making it seem like a losing proposition, it's essential to recognize that this perception is not entirely accurate. In fact, uncertainty is precisely what creates opportunities, making trading an exquisitely profitable endeavor for those who have successfully shifted their mindset from trying to predict every market movement to playing the numbers game. In other words, success comes to those traders who can consistently execute their well-defined trading strategy or system. Instead of aiming for perfection in each trade, they prioritize maintaining a positive expected value—a statistical concept that implies taking strategically sound trades that might not necessarily work individually but would squarely tilt the odds in their favor over time.

Now, this is simple in theory but challenging in practice. I know this all too well—embracing uncertainty is no easy feat; something about it strikes at our very core, deeply triggering us. If you want to get philosophical about it, maybe it's because uncertainty gives us existential dread and reminds us of our mortality. That is why we're caught in an endless cycle of craving certainty, even where it cannot exist. It gives us a sense of control over the absurdity of existence. Trading exemplifies this struggle exceptionally well. Most traders are inconsistent and unprofitable primarily because they are deeply intolerant of uncertainty; hence, they allow their emotions to dictate their decisions. They exhibit discipline and consistency when circumstances feel favorable, convenient, or motivating. They falter when faced with challenges, setbacks, or negative emotions. This "on and off" cycle keeps them tethered to mediocrity.

To do well as a trader, one needs not just a surface-level acceptance of uncertainty but a profound, soul-deep embrace of it. For me, getting to this point was a long and tedious journey that entailed acquiring new knowledge while unlearning old paradigms. I found myself frequently reassessing my entire worldview, enduring numerous highs and lows along the way. Admittedly, trading losses would affect me not only mentally but also spiritually, as muddled as this sounds. It was a lengthy process before I truly grasped, on a visceral level and not just intellectually, that one cannot conquer chaos; instead, one must surrender to it, embracing what I call "trading composure" through personal development. Therein lies the key.

In pursuing my trading dreams, I faced storms I had never anticipated—storms that weren't on any chart or in any market prediction model. They were internal tempests, fueled by overconfidence, underconfidence, despair, impatience, anger, and so on. It was during these tumultuous times that the significance of composure became crystal clear to me. As someone who appears calm and composed externally, composure had to mean something more, something deeper. It had to transcend mere surface appearances or even the archaic notion of "trading without emotions," as frequently touted by some traders. As I discovered, composure is about maintaining clarity, perspective, and emotional stability in an ongoing way amidst the ups and downs of the market or life. To be more specific, it is the radical noninterference with the natural flow of sensory experiences. For instance, if emotions arise in response to market fluctuations, rather than ignoring them or pushing them down, you adopt an observer stance, allowing them to arise and dissipate naturally. By practicing composure—indeed, it is a practice—you cultivate a capacity to avoid impulsive reactions. This detachment, or sangfroid, as the French would say, enables actions aligned with core values rather than transient emotions or wavering convictions.

Through numerous highs and lows, the market repeatedly showed me how it distributes profits to a select few. However, some lessons take time to sink in; thus, the market reiterated these teachings until they became deeply embedded in my consciousness. As I contemplate my journey—from zero to managing a multi-million-dollar fund—a smile creeps onto my face as I replay the profound changes and growth I've undergone. While some core essence of "me" seems unchanging, my beliefs, desires, and perspectives have evolved significantly over the years. Previously, my mindset wasn't calibrated for trading; I grappled with a fear of change and uncertainty, which led to impulsive tendencies. Over time, I've acquired wisdom in embracing uncertainty, and while my composure is still a work in progress, it's better than it's ever been. Intrinsically, most traders simply don't possess the right mindset for trading, and this not only dims their performance but also casts a shadow over their overall well-being. Sure, one could have the drive and requisite intelligence; one might even be naturally diligent and cool-headed. Still, that doesn't necessarily mean that they possess a mindset that is calibrated for the realities of this game. In this book, we'll explore what it means to have such a mindset; we'll also see how to develop it.

Trading is a game one plays against oneself. While anyone can analyze the market and devise trading strategies to gain a statistical edge, the matter of who actually comes out with consistent profits is often decided by their mindset. To emerge as a consistently profitable trader in the long term, one must exhibit utmost dedication to honing their craft and mastering their mind, starting with confronting their fear of uncertainty. My aim is not merely to guide you toward realizing your potential as a trader but also to facilitate personal growth in every facet of your life, albeit in my own modest capacity. Within the pages of this book, I will provide you with an exhaustive and meticulously crafted blueprint for cultivating trading composure. Together, we will delve into its fundamental essence and the profound transformative potential it holds. You will gain insights into fostering greater consistency in your trading endeavors and overall life journey. While I cannot guarantee immediate

financial success, I assure you that by comprehending and imple-
menting the principles I outline, you will undoubtedly evolve into a
more proficient trader and, overall, a better "you." Consequently,
you will enhance your trading journey with each step forward,
gradually positioning yourself among the elite group of traders who
achieve consistent profitability.

Foreword

In the tumultuous world of trading, where fortunes can pivot on the turn of a chart candle, there's one constant that often goes understated: the power of a composed mind. It's this very essence that the pages of *Trading Composure* seek to distill for its readers. As the voices behind the mic at *Chat with Traders* podcast, Ian Cox, my co-host, and I have engaged with the sharpest trading minds out there, and there is no doubt that this book is a standout.

The author, Yvan Byeajee, who we have had the pleasure of interviewing on the podcast, brings a wealth of knowledge and experience to the table, unpacking the psychological toolkit needed for trading from a perspective that is unique and important. This isn't your typical Trading Psychology book—it's deep, beautifully written, and action-oriented with a more introspective look at the mental game of trading.

As a fellow trader, navigating the ups and downs of the market for years now, *Trading Composure* hits home. It's the mentor I needed at a pivotal point in my trading journey, offering insights that meet me where I am and where I want to be.

Trading Composure holds the keys to a truly grounded, thoughtful, and practical approach to shift your mindset so that you can become mentally stronger and equipped to grow into a consistently profitable trader.

I invite you, fellow trader, to approach *Trading Composure* not merely as a book, but as a companion on your journey. Allow it to challenge you, to change you.

To your success in trading and life,
Tessa Dao
Producer and Co-Host of *Chat with Traders* podcast

If you know the way broadly, you will see it in everything.
—Miyamoto Musashi

Chapter 1
From Zero to Hero

Modest Origins

The sun is starting to set as I pen down this paragraph. I'm currently on the tropical isle of Mauritius in the Indian Ocean—a landmass roughly half the size of Rhode Island. It is winter at the moment, but that doesn't mean much here as the average yearly temperatures hover around 26°C (76°F). I'm sitting on the beach, in a quiet spot, and beneath me, the sand is a radiant gold, plush yet with a tactile crunch. The water before me is tantalizingly warm, clear, and painted in multiple hues of turquoise. I am currently experiencing what can only be described as a spiritual experience. I feel blessed to be here; I am connected to my breath, I am mindful of every moment, and as I contemplate my life, an immense feeling of gratitude overtakes my being.

Trading has allowed me to experience a level of freedom in life that most people can only dream of. But things weren't always like this; I struggled a lot before I became a consistent trader. In my early days, I grappled with many setbacks and hurdles that almost broke my spirit. Those daunting periods, filled with uncertainty, self-doubt, and tears, continue to resonate deeply with me, but as

1

I reflect on my journey, I've come to a profound realization. These seemingly insurmountable challenges, though harsh, served a grander purpose. In hindsight, they were not just obstacles; they were opportunities that shed light on my weaknesses, compelling me to change, grow, and prove to myself what I'm made of.

"Pain is the best teacher." I love this old saying, not because it is simply true but because it encapsulates the idea that we often find the impetus to change and adapt in our moments of deepest discomfort and distress. From my stance, I feel profoundly grateful for the pain that helped shape the trader I am today and the person I've become; it's something I wouldn't exchange for the world. Every moment paves the way for personal growth, and I'm continually learning to value life's teachings. For instance, right now as I'm writing this, in an almost comical twist, a random dog is relieving itself about a meter away from where I'm seated, and the stench is overpowering! Even in moments like this, there are lessons to be learned.

But let's go back a bit to the beginning of my journey toward trading composure. We all come to trading with our own story. My journey started in 1997; I was 17 years old, and the dot-com bubble was beginning to inflate. Everywhere I turned, it seemed like the world was buzzing about stocks, technology, and this new thing called the Internet. I grew up in the suburbs of Paris, France, and life there wasn't exactly a piece of cake. Picture this: a cramped apartment, four siblings, and an overwhelmed single mother struggling to keep the family afloat on welfare. That was my world. My mother also struggled with a mental health condition that wasn't formally diagnosed back then, leaving her without the necessary support to manage it effectively. Hence, her psychotic phases made life incredibly hard for my siblings and me, as we were often on the receiving end of it. The constant uncertainty and confusion, the emotional rollercoaster, the recurring conflicts and tensions—those were an almost everyday reality for us. Hence, growing up, we weren't the most well-adjusted human beings. For instance, I developed a stutter and a learning difficulty, to say nothing of limiting beliefs, and those became the chains anchoring my potential in life.

As a teenager, I withdrew more and more into myself. At school, the library became my refuge, shielding me from the relentless noise, bullying, and typical chaos of high school recess. But secluding myself from the world wasn't all that negative; in fact, it exposed me to the world of books. I was never a big reader to begin with. Instead, I had a habit of browsing, occasionally pausing to read a few passages without truly immersing myself in an entire book. This method of skimming, though unconventional, led me to stumble upon gems of wisdom, diverse perspectives, and intriguing narratives.

One day, a particular title caught my eye. It wasn't only the title that drew me in but also the book's condition. Worn and barely holding together, it seemed like the kind of book that had been donated to the school, as was often the case. The book was *How I Made $2 Million in the Stock Market* by Nicolas Darvas. As I began delving into its content, I found myself irresistibly pulled into Darvas's world. His narrative was a captivating blend of personal experiences, calculated risks, and a relentless pursuit of success amidst the ever-volatile stock market landscape. The book became the first one I ever immersed myself in from start to finish. Day by day, I would devour its pages, sometimes at the library, sometimes at home in the sanctuary of my room; it became my bible and took pride of place on my bedside table. Each night, with the powerful chords and lyrics of Guns N' Roses reverberating through my Walkman headphones, I'd lose myself in its pages. This ritual gave me great comfort, especially during the nights when the weight of my mother's psychotic episodes bore down on the household. The book was more than just a read; it was my refuge.

Being the young, wet-behind-the-ears fellow that I was, what fascinated me most was not the underlying principles and discipline that steered Darvas's decisions but rather the irresistible appeal of fast financial gains. This allure overshadowed everything else in the book, as I found myself daydreaming about replicating the man's success. In those moments, wrapped in the comforting dream of making it in the world of finances, I felt distanced from the chaos that unraveled around me. Darvas's success story of mastering the stock market painted a world of possibilities—a stark contrast to the unpredictability I was surrounded by in my life. My grasp on financial markets was tenuous at best; still, the allure of making a living through calculated risks gripped me, even if I couldn't articulate the specifics. I saw myself in Darvas, and this was enough to fan the flames of ambition within me.

My high school grades, however, painted a different picture. They were dropping quicker than a stock in freefall. Every red mark and low score was a reminder that I wasn't thriving in that environment. I felt out of place in a conventional educational system that didn't cater to my unique ways of processing information. Teachers, classmates, and even family made me feel "less than" for being a slow learner—but it's not that I lack intelligence; rather, I absorb information differently and on my own terms. Yet, they all saw my pace as a deficiency rather than a different rhythm, and sadly, their perceptions and comments began to wear on me; I began internalizing their beliefs, doubting my own capabilities, and eventually, I dropped out of high school.

As I drifted through life, my journey was punctuated by an array of odd jobs, but nothing that genuinely ignited a passion within me or hinted at a lasting career. I've always had a stutter; back then, it was particularly pronounced. This condition, combined with my struggles with social anxiety, made job interviews daunting affairs. Consistent employment eluded me, adding another layer of hardship to my already tumultuous life. A few years later, as the Internet gained wider adoption in society, connectivity increased among people, and information was getting shared at a pace never seen before. Amid this tech revolution, online trading was carving its niche, heralding a new era of financial possibilities. One day, my older brother, who was always a step ahead in the tech curve, called me into his room to show me a financial website. The computer screen was awash with financial quotes, numbers, and news headlines as he remarked, "Check this out—some guys are pulling in millions just by trading stocks. They sit on their butt all day and press a few buttons. Crazy, right?" Feigning surprise, I nodded, though deep down, the spark from years ago rekindled.

In the era of Nicolas Darvas, day trading as we know it today was a foreign concept. The technological limitations of the time and the structure of financial markets didn't allow for the rapid buying and selling of securities within a single trading day. Darvas operated in a market environment where trading was more about strategic holding based on longer-term analyses and cues. However, the trading landscape underwent a seismic shift with the advent of the Internet and its subsequent integration into financial systems. The connectivity, real-time data, and tools made available by the Internet gave birth to this new style of trading, which allowed traders to capitalize on minute-to-minute (sometimes even second-to-second) price shifts. Obviously, I was immediately gripped by the possibilities. The world of trading, it seemed, was calling me once again. Here was a field where my stutter and distinct learning rhythm didn't matter. Trading was an arena in which I knew I could succeed. I often joke that it has done for me what years of schooling couldn't—it ignited a burning passion within me. In the market, it isn't about how fluently you speak or how good you are at office politics. Fundamentally, what matters is astute observation, keen analysis, and the ability to make thoughtful and strategic choices. In light of that, my surface-level "weaknesses" were almost irrelevant; I intuited that trading would allow me to reshape the disempowering narratives I had believed about myself for so long.

At that time, every corner I turned, the world seemed abuzz with chatter about tech stocks, so my curiosity naturally gravitated toward how to trade them. While today's digital age boasts a plethora of online resources to guide budding traders, quality trading education was a rarity during that period. To learn, you typically had to attend seminars or voraciously consume books. Unfortunately, high-priced seminars were beyond my budget, which led me to join a local trading and investment club. Every Thursday after work, I'd find myself among seasoned traders and savvy investors, absorbing invaluable technical insights and strategies they generously shared. I also bought myself a copy of Nicolas Darvas's book—the one I picked up at my school library a few years ago—and re-read it numerous times. The man's story was a tremendous source of inspiration and motivation for me then. Equally, I spent countless hours poring over financial websites, deciphering financial quotes, and navigating the dense influx of market information. I recall one particular element that grabbed my attention—a compound return table (see Table 1.1). As I began to grasp the formidable power of compounding, it dawned on me that the dream of becoming a millionaire within a realistic time frame wasn't a pipe dream; that ideal seemed tantalizingly attainable, and my pulse raced as I envisioned the boundless opportunities.

Yet, amidst this whirlwind of aspirations, the reality of my day job persisted. But its mundane routine was now juxtaposed against a fervent goal: I was unwavering in my quest to trade for a living. The vision of bidding adieu to conventional jobs became increasingly vivid in my mind. In the iconic movie *Scarface*, there's a scene where the protagonist, Tony Montana, drenched in frustration for his thankless service at a Miami eatery, dramatically throws his greasy apron at his boss in a bold act of defiance (De Palma 1983, 0:18:35). The intensity of that moment, where Montana decides he's worth more than the petty world he's confined to, resonated deeply with me. I longed for my own moment of liberation, to break free from the constraints of my dull and unfulfilling job, just as Montana had done with his, and each day, that scene from the movie played in my head with heightened clarity.

Time rolled on, and eventually, I reached a pivotal moment where I was finally ready to take the leap of faith, ready to make the

Table 1.1   A compound return table showcasing the substantial effects that both the return rate and the length of the investment period have on the expansion of a $10,000 trading account.

Years	5% Return	6% Return	10% Return	11% Return	15% Return	20% Return
2	$11,025	$11,326	$12,100	$12,321	$13,225	$14,400
5	$12,726.82	$13,382.26	$16,105.1	$16,850.58	$20,113.57	$24,883.2
7	$14,071	$15,036.30	$19,487.17	$20,761.60	$26,600.20	$35,831.81
10	$16,288.95	$17,908.48	$25,937.42	$28,394.21	$40,455.58	$61,917.36
12	$17,958.56	$20,121.96	$31,384.28	$34,984.51	$53,502.50	$89,161.00
15	$20,789.28	$23,965.58	$41,772.48	$47,845.89	$81,370.62	$154,070.22

magic happen, ready to bank millions, just like my hero, Darvas. The year was 2006, and I quit my final job as a count team member in a casino. The very next day, I transferred all my savings to a trading account. A few days later, I was up and running; a new chapter of my life had begun, and I was all in.

Almost Within Grasp, Yet Elusive

As the story unfolds, what transpired next is a series of events I'd equate to a haunting nightmare. My account plummeted in my inaugural trading year, witnessing a gut-wrenching 60% drawdown. This was absolutely brutal; it felt like the floor had disappeared beneath me, and my confidence was shattered. Understand, I wasn't navigating blind. I had a well-crafted trading system, the result of insightful conversations I had with fellow traders from the investment club I frequented and countless hours spent researching, fine-tuning, and testing against historical data. In terms of capital, I also had enough of it, at least a hundred thousand dollars that I saved over the years. Thus, I had the tools and the means to facilitate success, and every day, like tantalizing mirages on the horizon, the market dangled promises of unprecedented wealth right before my eyes. Yet, when it came to seizing these golden opportunities, my feet turned to clay, paralyzed by the ever-looming specter of emotions. I faltered at the very brink of success.

My response to uncertainty was amateurish at best; I was fraught with indecision and recklessness. Short-term trades turned into long-term investments and vice versa, a murky blending of strategies that no seasoned trader would endorse. Like a moth drawn to a flame, I found myself impulsively frequenting trade-call forums trying to catch a mover that would 100x my money. My gaze flitted nervously across the screen, toggling between time frames, desperately seeking a semblance of certainty in a landscape that inherently defies it. Rather than cutting my losses, I clung stubbornly to sinking positions, pouring more capital into them as if sheer will could turn the tide. Blindly, I defied the market's rhythm, going long when all signs screamed bearish and short when the bulls ran rampant. Those are all moves that any savvy investor will warn you against, yet I made them all, and many times over.

Each trading session was a tumultuous carousel of emotions. The ebb and flow of wins and losses was mentally taxing—triumphs inflated my ego, while failures gnawed at my soul. My behavioral patterns and mental game weren't conducive to success in trading, and I wasn't even aware of that. I didn't even begin to suspect that the problem was me, the operator, the man behind the wheel. So, at some point, even though my original trading system was perfectly fine, I began tweaking it. I incorporated derivative instruments like options unplanningly, without the due diligence they demanded. And when that didn't yield expected results, I started chasing some illusory holy grail trading system, of course, spending a fortune doing so while never finding anything.

On a serendipitous afternoon, as if guided by fate, I wandered into my local bookstore. There, nestled among other tomes, was *The Disciplined Trader* by Mark Douglas. Intrigued, I took it home, immersing myself in its pages. As I delved deeper, a profound clarity began to seep in. Trading, as Douglas articulated, was not just about numbers or strategies; it was a dance of emotions, a test of self-control and mental fortitude. Though I had previously encountered this idea of "trading psychology" in the works of Nicolas Darvas, it hadn't truly resonated. Perhaps, in our journey through life, we only see what we're prepared to see; we comprehend only what aligns with our existing beliefs.

With every page of *The Disciplined Trader*, I felt a seismic shift in my perspective. Seeds of hope long buried beneath layers of despair began to germinate in the recesses of my mind. Galvanized by Douglas's insights, particularly his emphasis on probabilistic thinking and the individuality of each trade, I found myself reevaluating my mental game. No longer was I glued to the screens, agonizing over every fluctuation. I placed my trades with a newfound conviction, then stepped back, allowing the market to take its course. My thinking evolved, anchored more in probabilities than whims. My expectations became more realistic, grounded in a commitment to discipline. Bit by bit, my confidence, which had once been shattered, began to rebuild. Remarkably, within a span of five months, my trading performance, once awash in red, transformed. I was on the cusp of recouping all my losses; but then, the 2008 financial collapse started unrolling.

Generally, maneuvering through bull markets is relatively "easy"—they tend to be more forgiving since they are predominantly fueled by emotions like greed and complacency, which inflate asset values across the board, providing a wider margin for decisional errors. Bear markets, however, are fueled by panic and fear; hence, they are more vicious and unpredictable. Thus, the real test for a trader worth their salt is to navigate such intricate market landscapes not necessarily profitably but with ongoing stability of mind to better protect their capital and past accumulated profits. Regrettably, I failed to uphold that basic rule. When the market turned, so did my mindset. My impulsiveness reared its ugly head again, and slowly, my life savings, which I had audaciously poured into my trading account, began to evaporate before my eyes. Witnessing the slow bleed of what I held dear, my resolve crumbled.

In the aftermath of embracing Mark Douglas's insights, I thought I had found my panacea. Yet, as the days unfurled, it became evident that those changes were mere plasters over gaping wounds. Beneath the facade of newfound understanding lurked the same old emotional and impulsive me. My unskillful states were just there waiting to resurface, and they did. Weeks, sometimes months, of consistent profitability were now punctuated by massive drawdowns because, somewhere down the line, I always found a way to lose my stability of mind. Any slight perturbation and I'd spiral into a vortex of irrationality.

Desperate for answers, I revisited Douglas's wisdom. But this time, I also sought solace in a plethora of other resources on trading psychology. The quest for a holy grail had reignited within me, only now it wasn't a fail-proof system I was after but a potent elixir to quell my tempestuous psychological storms. From the esoteric realms of Neuro-linguistic programming (NLP) and hypnosis to the introspective corridors of psychotherapy, I delved deep, seeking a way out of my unproductive ways. Some avenues offered glimmers of hope, others led to dead ends, but none provided the transformational change I yearned for. They merely offered temporary reprieves, not addressing the root of my psychological quagmire. Over five tumultuous years, the market—aided by my inner demons—devoured nearly $100,000 of my savings. That sum meant a lot to me at that time since it represented dreams, aspirations, and countless sacrifices. The weight of those losses bore heavily on my psyche; the mental toll was truly debilitating.

As days turned into weeks and weeks into months, the weight of my out-of-hand losses and failures grew ever heavier on my shoulders. The rooms of my home seemed dimmer, and my interactions with people, even close ones, seemed more strained. The few friends and family I had watched powerlessly as I withdrew more and more, pushed to the precipice of an engulfing abyss of despair.

Rock Bottom

"How did it come to this?" The surreal haze of disbelief enveloped me. In a breathless moment, I whispered to myself, "I'm done!" And in that echoing silence, it wasn't just the world of trading I wanted to abandon, but the very thread of life itself. The weight of desolation bore down on me. Days merged into nights as I neglected the man in the mirror. The sharpness of my jawline emerged, testimony to the meals skipped and the weight shed. Shadows deepened beneath my eyes, painting the grim portrait of a soul unhinged. The gnawing emptiness wasn't just a result of financial despair; it stemmed from the wounds of my childhood, wounds that failure rubbed salt into. Each setback felt like a reaffirmation of the inadequacies I had battled since my younger days.

As said earlier, I grew up cradling the erratic moods of a mentally unstable parent. The ground beneath me seldom felt solid; the sanctity of routine and predictability was a luxury I rarely knew. Every day brought adversity, shame, pain—things could turn sour in the blink of an eye; any moment could explode into chaos.

The relentless stresses of my formative years weren't the kind that fostered growth or resilience; instead, they were a relentless grind, always on the precipice of breaking me apart. Consider this: In nature, diamonds are birthed from carbon exposed to extreme pressures deep within the Earth's mantle. In the right measure, this pressure can transform a simple element into one of the most beautiful and sought-after gems in the world. But even in this natural marvel, there's a delicate balance—too little pressure and the carbon remains unaltered; too much pressure and it's crushed, never getting the chance to metamorphose. Drawing a parallel to my own life, the pressures of my childhood were excessive, nearly shattering the essence of who I was. I felt more like carbon being crushed rather than shaped and refined. The potential diamond within me was at risk of being lost forever, subdued by the immense stresses that sought to define my existence. To survive, I crafted a set of coping mechanisms—I became adept at reading the room, anticipating storms, and sometimes, when things got too intense, retreating into the safety of my shell, curling up, and making myself invisible.

As I stepped into the world of trading, the volatile nature of markets strangely echoed the unpredictability of my childhood. But this time, the old coping defenses would not suffice. Trading demands a surrender to uncertainty, a willingness to embrace the rawness of vulnerability, and accept losses as lessons, things I had never really grasped. No longer could I hide or recoil at the signs of danger, yet, time and again, I did exactly that. Even as my logical mind and trading knowledge urged me to act differently, my emotional self overrode those cues, which became the root of my undoing. It wasn't just about the money lost; it was the mental turmoil that took a toll on me. It was my inability to break free from automatic responses that put me in a catastrophic position. The market, in its brutal honesty, mirrors back to us our deepest fears and insecurities, and in my case, it held up a magnifying glass to the fractures in my psyche that had been long glossed over. And yet, amidst this bleakness, the irony wasn't lost on me. Here I stood, teetering on the edge of what I had once envisioned as my ultimate dream. Instead of the anticipated euphoria of accomplishment, an oppressive weight threatened to pull me into the abyss. All my tools, all my preparation, and yet, the magnitude of my reality was paralyzingly overwhelming.

During one of these bleak evenings, I had an unexpected visit from an old friend from the investment club I used to be part of, Francois. Though Francois had amassed a staggering wealth from trading commodity futures, his appearance was disarmingly unassuming. Dressed in simple attire, he exuded a quiet humility. To the untrained eye, he could easily be mistaken for just another face in the crowd, his multi-millionaire status hidden behind a veil of modesty. We settled in a coffee shop down the street, steam curling up from freshly brewed expresso cups. The silence was comfortable, but the weight of my experiences pressed on my chest. Soon, the floodgates opened; I found myself recounting the highs and lows and the mistakes and lessons of my trading journey. Francois sat across from me, his steady gaze absorbing every word with an understanding only a fellow trader could offer. He didn't interrupt, only nodding occasionally, allowing me to navigate the labyrinth of my emotions, laying them bare. Over cups of steaming coffee, we talked—or rather, I spilled the story of my tumultuous journey while he listened, patient and empathetic. Francois spoke of balance and the importance of grounding oneself, not just in trading, but in life. "You're more than your trades, more than the numbers on a screen," he'd said, "The market is just one facet of a multifaceted life." His words struck a chord. I had become so engrossed in the volatile world of trading that I lost sight of the bigger picture. My identity, self-worth, and happiness became inextricably tied to the market and my trading performance.

Following that heart-to-heart, I took a sabbatical from trading. I reconnected with the hobbies I'd once loved, like hiking. I could barely get myself to look at my trading account because I was so afraid of what I would see there. At one point, I went to a park and sat on a bench. Summer had just ended; leaves were starting to fall, and the area, usually lively and colorful, was deserted and bleak, echoing the desolation I felt within. However, amidst this gloomy setting, I witnessed something remarkable. A squirrel, poised to leap from a thin branch, launched itself into the air, traversing the daunting space between two trees. Its tiny frame, balanced on such a fragile twig moments before, now showcased an awe-inspiring blend of agility and grace. It dawned on me that these creatures operated on pure instinct—their every move was dictated not by deliberate calculations but by an innate sense of the odds. As I watched the squirrel's graceful leap, I realized that this seemingly mundane moment was a profound lesson in dealing with uncertainty. In its daily quest for sustenance, this squirrel constantly faced the unpredictable challenges of nature, from potential predators to rapidly changing environmental conditions. And yet, here it was, taking a risk with such finesse and confidence. This observation became the catalyst for my evolving thoughts on uncertainty.

The squirrel doesn't possess a conscious understanding of risk as we humans do. It doesn't weigh options or overanalyze situations. It instinctively evaluates its environment, processes information in real time, and acts based on its instinctual understanding of the odds. Again, it's not a calculation; it's an innate knowing. For the squirrel, life is a continual dance with uncertainty, and its survival hinges on its ability to adapt and respond effectively. In the world of the squirrel, uncertainty isn't a burden but an integral part of existence. While it's true that every jump or decision it makes doesn't guarantee safety or success, the squirrel doesn't get paralyzed by fear. Instead, it embraces uncertainty as a natural state of being, focusing on the present moment, gathering all its energy and intent into that singular leap.

This observation led me to ponder my own relationship with uncertainty. In the trading world, I was often overwhelmed by the unpredictability and volatility of the markets. But if a squirrel could tackle its world of uncertainty with such aplomb, surely there are lessons I could learn here. Instead of perceiving uncertainty as an adversary, could I—like the squirrel—see it as a constant companion, a force to be acknowledged and respected but not feared? The squirrel's behavior became an allegory, urging me to reconsider my views on the market and, more broadly, on life. I had a sprouting realization that embracing uncertainty and operating within its confines with agility, rather than overthinking and overanalyzing, could be the key to success. It's not about eliminating uncertainty but learning to dance with it, just like the squirrel.

I further realized that top-tier traders are detached from the emotional rollercoaster of trading. They respect the boundless opportunities in the market but are firmly anchored in the disciplined execution of their strategies. By emphasizing probabilities over possibilities, they remain grounded, their emotions in check, echoing the squirrel's unwavering focus. The age-old adage warns against emotional trading, but as sentient beings, how do we transcend our inherent emotional nature without going through a lobotomy? Emotions form our very core, as inseparable as our heartbeat. Hence, the key lies not in suppressing emotions but in minimizing their influence. And the first step toward this detachment is adopting a probabilistic mindset. It wasn't that I was unfamiliar with this concept; instead, I had failed to truly realize it. Sometimes, we stand too close to trees and can't see the forest.

During my sabbatical, I found solace in solitude, often amidst nature, reflecting on the trajectory of my life, its purpose, and my perpetual struggles with trading. A newfound companion during these introspective journeys was my journal. The act of penning down my thoughts and reflections provided clarity, transforming the abstract into tangible revelations. It became a conduit for self-awareness, a mirror reflecting my deepest fears, desires, and insights. As the days ebbed and flowed, my journal burgeoned with revelations, and naturally, I felt more and more compelled to emancipate myself from my internal shackles. While journaling provided a therapeutic release, what I discovered next was nothing short of transformational.

My Journey to Composure

Imagine I hand you a key; however, this isn't just any key—it unlocks a vault of unparalleled wisdom and clarity. Once turned, it sharpens your decision-making, calms your nerves, keeps impulsiveness at bay, and heightens your overall aptitude to respond wisely and measuredly. Beyond these riches, the vault also reveals more treasures: a surge in self-confidence, peace with your past, comfort with the mysteries of the future, a newfound trust in yourself, and so much more. The best part? This key isn't forged from gold or silver but from something far more invaluable and pure. It won't cost you a dime, but it demands dedication: a commitment to use it every day of your life. Are you intrigued? Would you use such a key? Well, this key is the profound practice of meditation.

Amidst the myriad habits and routines I've adopted over the years, if there was one singular practice that has profoundly shaped my journey, especially in the ruthless realm of the markets, it would be meditation. This ancient, timeless ritual has not only centered my being; it has become the very compass guiding my decisions and actions in life. I wasn't introduced to meditation by anyone; instead, I stumbled upon it almost by mistake. Every so often, especially during the quieter moments of my day, I found myself gravitating toward a unique solace. Without any prior instruction or understanding, I would simply lay down, close my eyes, and drift inward. It wasn't a practice I was taught or something I had consciously decided to adopt. It just happened naturally and organically. The world's clamor faded into the background when I sank into myself, replaced by a profound sense of presence and serenity. The overwhelming rush of thoughts, worries, and plans that usually consumed my mind dissipated. Instead, a refreshing spaciousness and clarity enveloped me. While I hadn't yet recognized it as "meditation," this innate, intuitive act offered a state of being I had never felt or experienced before.

One evening, bathed in the afterglow of one such impromptu session, a new curiosity took hold. With no clear intent, I found myself typing the words "meditation retreat" into a search engine. Scrolling through the results, my eyes settled on a serene image of a secluded retreat center enveloped by towering trees and mirrored by a calm lake. Something deep within nudged me toward it. I signed up on a whim, driven by a force that evaded explanation. I wasn't entirely sure what awaited me, nor did I have any preconceived notions of what a "retreat" entailed. All I knew was this inexplicable pull, this magnetic draw toward exploring, understanding, and deepening this newfound state of being.

Arriving at the retreat, every cell in my body felt aligned with this decision; however, as the days unfolded, unexpected challenges arose. Immersed in prolonged silence, the hours seemed to stretch endlessly. What's more, my years of sedentary living—sitting in front of a computer stalking the market for opportunities—had taken a toll on my body, leaving my lower back vulnerable and weak. And now, confined to the stillness of the meditation posture, every twinge and ache magnified. One particularly grueling session saw me caught in a whirlwind of torment, the pain so intense that silent tears streamed down my face. Emotionally and physically overwhelmed, I found myself at a breaking point. I got up and sought out the assistant teacher, ready to declare my intention to leave the retreat. But her calm, measured words halted me in my tracks: "If you choose to leave, that's your decision, and I respect it. However, before you go ahead with this decision, see if you can spend just one more day here. Reflect deeply on the nature of your discomfort. Observe it; see if you can discern how much of this pain is truly physical and how much is a construct of your mind." Skeptical, yet with a seed of curiosity planted, I returned to the cushion, silently vowing to depart the following dawn.

As the hours passed, a shift began to unfold. With every conscious breath, I delved deeper into the intricate dance of sensations, thoughts, and emotions, and gradually, the boundaries began to blur. Was the pain genuinely as insurmountable as it had seemed, or had my mind amplified and distorted it? The layers began to peel away, and an empowering realization dawned. While some pain was genuine, a significant portion was born from mental resistance, deeply rooted beliefs, and patterns of perception. The journey of deciphering between physical discomfort and mental constructs had just begun and promised profound insights and transformation.

With this newfound perspective, the subsequent days took on a different hue. Each meditation session became an exploration rather than an endurance test. I started to approach every pang and discomfort with curiosity, attempting to untangle the web of physical sensations from the threads of mental narratives that had previously dominated my experience. By viewing the pain through this lens of inquiry, it began to lose its vice-like grip on me. Moments of discomfort that previously felt eternal now seemed to ebb and flow like waves upon a shore. I recognized the impermanent nature of pain and, even more crucially, the impermanence of the stories my mind wove around it. The atmosphere of the retreat, the serene surroundings, the collective intent of all participants, all contributed to this evolving understanding. Shared meals became moments of reflection, and walks in nature turned into profound lessons on the interconnectedness of all things. Days melded into nights, and the retreat's end was soon in sight. However, by this point, my earlier desire to flee had vanished; instead, it was replaced by profound gratitude not just for the physical practice but for the invaluable lessons learned.

On the last day, we broke our silence. The peace, the clarity, and the transformative insights I had gathered were so precious that I felt an innate desire to dive deeper, to explore further, so I approached the assistant teacher, expressing my wish to extend my stay. "I've just begun to scratch the surface," I confided. "There's so much more I feel compelled to understand, and this place feels like the right environment to do so." She looked at me, her eyes reflecting a blend of wisdom and compassion, and then shared about the "sitting and serving program." This program allowed participants to continue their practice while also contributing to the daily operations of the retreat, creating a harmonious cycle of giving and receiving. Thus, my initial 10-day retreat transformed into a profound 2-month sojourn. Every day brought new revelations, deeper meditative experiences, and a growing bond with the retreat community. As I meditated, served meals, tended to the gardens, and participated in group discussions around the teachings and the philosophy behind the practice, I felt an unparalleled sense of purpose that nurtured my soul.

When I finally departed the retreat center, the world outside seemed different, as if I were seeing it through a newly polished

lens. But one thing was clear: my journey into the depths of meditation and its myriad philosophies had only begun. An insatiable
hunger to understand more—to delve deeper into the annals of this
ancient art—had taken root within me. Over the next four months,
my compass was guided by this thirst for knowledge. Maps and
travel plans became a testament to my quest, leading me to various
corners of the world. From the tranquil monasteries perched on the
mountaintops of Bhutan to the serene ashrams by the sacred Ganges
in India, every destination was a chapter in my unfolding saga of
discovery. Each location, each tradition, brought with it a unique
flavor of contemplative practice. While some places emphasized
rigorous discipline and strict adherence to timeworn techniques,
others championed a more fluid, intuitive approach to meditation.
There were places where silence reigned supreme, enveloping every
aspirant in its comforting embrace and others where chants and
mantras resonated through the air, creating an ethereal symphony
of devotion. Living in these monasteries, among monks who had
dedicated their entire lives to the practice, I was privy to a wealth of
knowledge. With them, I learned not just meditation techniques
but also the philosophy and wisdom behind those practices. Being
the curious mind that I am, I would often have hour-long discussions with fellow monks, spanning topics from the nature of the
self to the intricacies of the mind and the impermanence of everything. There was an unspoken bond, a shared understanding that,
despite our varied backgrounds and cultures, we were all seekers on
the same path, looking for answers to life's most profound questions.

Throughout this period of exploration, I found myself constantly reflecting on my experiences in trading and the many setbacks I faced in the market. I further realized that a significant part
of my struggle in trading wasn't just about making the right calls or
predicting market trends; it was deeply rooted in my difficulty in
confronting and truly accepting the inherent uncertainty of the
market. As days turned into weeks, this introspection deepened.
The serene environments of the monasteries and the wisdom shared
by fellow contemplatives provided a conducive setting for me to dissect my previous decisions, my reactions to losses, and my overall

mindset toward the market. It dawned on me that, much like meditation, trading, too, requires a balance of focus, detachment, and a deep understanding and acceptance of impermanence and chaos. In between sessions of meditation and teachings on ancient philosophies, I would often lie on my bed and juxtapose my past trading patterns with the newfound insights from this spiritual journey. I began to see correlations between my impulsive decisions in the market and the unchecked, reactive thoughts that the practice of meditation aimed to tame. The more I reflected, the clearer it became that my challenges in embracing uncertainty in trading mirrored the broader human struggle of accepting the unpredictable nature of life itself. As time passed, these reflections enriched my understanding of my past trading decisions. They laid the foundation for a renewed approach to markets, one that was more balanced, grounded, and in tune with the ebb and flow of both the market and life's uncertainties. Concepts that once seemed superficially understood now felt more integrated, like deeply rooted trees that had finally found nourishment in fertile soil. This newfound depth of understanding began to permeate every aspect of my life.

Life was good in these monasteries. Not luxurious by any means but peaceful and good. Life unfolded with a serene simplicity that belied its profound depth. Yet, as days turned into weeks and weeks into months, a persistent whisper echoed within the corridors of my mind: "You're running away from your true life." Though the monastic life held a certain allure, promising a horizon of eternal serenity, I found myself grappling with its implications. There was no denying the beauty of it: immersed in the study of the philosophy of mind, partaking in hours of introspection, diving deep into the intricacies of my psyche, and cultivating profound insights. Nestled away from the relentless hustle of modernity, this environment became a crucible for forging composure and peace. The monastic realm offered an idyllic existence, and I could have easily lived here for the rest of my life. Yet, with every sunrise, a nagging thought persisted: as profound as it was, the tranquility here felt almost too easy. It became clear that maintaining composure within these sacred walls was one thing, but could this serenity hold its ground amid the tempests of the "real world"? The real crucible, I realized, lay beyond these walls—in the unpredictable theater of everyday life where chaos, hardships, losses, conflicts, and uncertainties choreographed a relentless dance. It's one thing to remain zen when ensconced in solitude, but the true mettle of one's practice is tested amidst life's turbulent currents. There was an urgency for me to take this cultivated wisdom and apply it to the "real world," to the cacophonies of daily existence, to the unpredictable ebb and flow of emotions, to the very core of humanity's shared experience. I yearned to know: can inner tranquility withstand life's fiercest storms? Embracing this epiphany, I returned to the familiar yet now-altered landscape of my "ordinary life," ready to navigate its labyrinth with the tools and insights from my monastic sojourn.

Upon my return, the rhythm of the world I once knew had changed—or perhaps it was I who had transformed? But now, I was out of a job, and the necessity to sustain myself weighed heavily like a cloak reminding me of real-world responsibilities. But the crucible of my time in the monastery had imbued me with a treasure more valuable than gold: a renewed perspective and an enriched mindset. Gazing upon the vast expanse of possibilities, I felt an old spark reignite within. The world of trading, which had once been a maze of confusion and setbacks, beckoned again. Yet, this time, I vowed to approach it not as a mere player but as a sage armed with insights from a journey beyond the mundane. Drawing from the depths of my newfound wisdom, I waded back into the tumultuous waters of the market. As I plucked the courage to glance at my trading account, the numbers staring back were a stark reminder of past battles—from an original investment of $100,000, only $14,000 remained. However, to me, this wasn't a number of defeat anymore; it stood as a symbol of resilience, of lessons learned and of the potential to begin anew. And perhaps above all, it was a test, for if I could grow this amount consistently and predictably, it would confirm the transformation I underwent.

Lo and behold, that is precisely what happened. With every trade, I embodied a dance of strategy and equanimity, blending analytical precision with the serene detachment I had cultivated.

Setbacks, while inevitable, no longer shook my core. Instead, they were lessons, echoes from the market teaching me its ever-evolving rhythm. The emotional rollercoasters of past trading days were replaced with a poised equilibrium, grounding me even in the face of challenges. As weeks turned to months and months into years, the growth of my trading account was not just monetary but symbolic. It was a testament to the profound importance of inner transformation.

The failure rate is high among traders. There are many chart analysts out there but very few consistently profitable traders. It's not an exaggeration—the number of consistently profitable traders is astonishingly low (Rolf 2019). If trading were merely a matter of chart analysis and deciphering patterns, we would see a greater success rate. However, this is far from reality. Beneath the surface-level complexities of graphs and data lies an even more intricate challenge: the ever-present cloud of uncertainty. Markets, by their very nature, are chaotic, and this inherent uncertainty often clashes with our deep-rooted desire for stability and control. Coming to terms with this uncertainty isn't just about intellectual acceptance. It's a profound psychological shift requiring more than just analytical skills. Embracing this uncertainty and learning to dance in its ebb and flow requires specialized training, transcending traditional chart analysis, and diving deep into the recesses of one's psyche. Only by mastering this can one hope to thrive in the chaotic world of trading.

As I draw this reflection on my life's journey to a close, I believe there's power in sharing our struggles and triumphs. Offering you this snapshot into the winding path of my pursuit of composure isn't just about transparency; it's about kindling a beacon of hope and possibility for you. My own hope is that in my experiences, you see a mirror to your potential and the affirmation that greatness isn't the preserve of a select few. In the vast realm of trading, where my name now resonates with some measure of recognition, it's essential to understand that my beginnings were as ordinary as they come. Far from the plush comforts of inherited wealth or privilege, my journey has been one marked by trials and tribulations.

The confinements of traditional education did not suit me, leading to an early departure from high school. In addition, grappling with a learning difficulty meant that my path to knowledge often deviated from the norm. However, within this perceived disadvantage lay my strength. Fueled by an unparalleled commitment, unwavering passion, and a relentless drive, I approach challenges with genuine sincerity. When I encountered the world of trading, it wasn't just another endeavor for me; it became an all-consuming passion, a vocation I pursued with every fiber of my being.

In retrospect, it's fascinating how the universe orchestrates this path for me. I'm very fortunate and grateful to be in the position that I'm in today. Currently, I'm managing a multi-million-dollar fund for myself and on behalf of a small group of investors. And perhaps the better part of it is that I'm doing this from the comfort of my home. Admittedly, I'm not the best trader that ever lived; far from it. However, I'm exquisitely consistent. Some days I win, some days I lose, but in totality, my gains substantially eclipse any losses incurred resulting in a steadily rising equity curve that is a testament to the viability of my strategies and the strength of my composure. With trading occupying only a fraction of my time, I dedicate my off-hours to guiding serious traders through the transformative journey of recalibrating their mindset for trading.

I've always considered myself a private individual, not one who naturally gravitates toward the public eye. Social interactions have always been a challenge for me, marked by a level of awkwardness I've been working hard to overcome for as long as I can remember. Additionally, as mentioned earlier, I've always spoken with a stutter, a condition that has, in many ways, shaped my preference for privacy and introspection over public discourse. When I first began sharing my insights on trading psychology online, it was a modest endeavor, more of a personal outlet than a quest for recognition. The thought that my musings and experiences would resonate with a broader audience seemed far-fetched. To my surprise, what started as a small personal project blossomed into something much larger and more impactful than I could have imagined. As my online presence grew, so did the attention. I found myself with an audience that was not only interested in what I had to say but also found a reflection of their own struggles in my journey. The influx of emails from traders worldwide, many of whom were grappling with similar challenges, was overwhelming. Hundreds of messages poured in every month, each sharing personal stories of struggles and seeking guidance. My unexpected foray into the public eye didn't stop there. I began receiving invitations to appear on popular trading podcasts, participate in radio interviews, and contribute to well-respected media outlets. Opportunities arose to speak at events, often alongside esteemed experts in the trading and investing world. I had never sought out this level of public engagement, and frankly, it was quite daunting, considering my innate preference for privacy and my struggles with social interaction. However, despite the discomfort and the challenges this posed to my personal nature, I felt a compelling sense of duty to continue this path. Helping struggling traders became more than just a casual pursuit; it turned into a responsibility, one that was deeply intertwined with my own search for meaning and purpose.

I firmly believe that trading is a mental game. It is a game one plays against oneself. Unfortunately, most traders ignore that; they only pay attention to charts, and that's a big mistake. I, too, was guilty of that: I believed trading was all about finding the right strategy. In reality, trading is mainly about becoming the right person—someone who consistently acts in their own best interest. Realizing that potential isn't just about desire; it requires dedicated effort and an ongoing commitment to growth. So much more is possible than what you're currently getting; so much more awaits you in terms of growth and success if you have your heart and mind in the right places. And I don't doubt that you do! But then, it's about doing the work and starting the journey to composure.

A Three-Pillar Approach to Composure

This book doesn't pretend to be anything; it's simply a collection of thoughts, experiences, and insights from my years of trading and working with traders in my coaching practice. I give you things as they are and as I currently understand them. I am not portraying myself as something I'm not; I don't have big diplomas or technical jargon to impress you. In writing this book, my goal wasn't to boost my ego but to be helpful by shedding light on the mindset and behavior required to excel in an uncertainty-ridden field like trading. Within the book's pages, I've distilled years of observations, personal experiences, and lessons from fellow traders into insights that will illuminate your path. I shed light on how trading isn't just a test of your analytical skills but also a reflection of your mental landscape. My goal is to help bridge the gap between the technical aspects of trading and the emotional challenges that often overshadow them. With the insights and lessons captured in these pages, you'll embark on a journey of self-discovery and growth, enabling you to approach trading not just as a financial endeavor but as a holistic pursuit of personal and professional mastery.

My original choice for the title of this book was *Riding Uncertainty: Insights from a Consistent Trader*. However, I felt compelled to choose a title that more aptly depicted the profound personal transformation required to excel in the realm of trading. Hence, *Trading Composure: Mastering Your Mind for Trading Success* became a natural choice. This composure I keep alluding to is multifaceted and nuanced. It is more than just a stoic facade; it goes beyond the mere robotic execution of trades. At its core, composure embodies a profound inner resilience, a steadfastness of mind that transcends the fluctuations of the market or life. It is the ability to remain grounded amidst chaos, to approach each trade with clarity and equanimity, regardless of external circumstances, in an ongoing manner. It entails radical acceptance of the natural flow of sensory experiences, whatever they are and however long they last. For instance, when emotions arise in response to market fluctuations, rather than suppressing or ignoring them, one adopts an observer stance, allowing them to arise and dissipate naturally. This avoids impulsive reactions, enabling actions aligned with core values rather than transient emotions or wavering convictions.

It's crucial to distinguish composure from what is often perceived as "the zone," a state of heightened focus popularized by figures like Mark Douglas. "The zone," however blissful it is, is a temporary state, typically achieved under specific conditions or circumstances. Composure, on the other hand, is enduring and not reliant on external factors. It is not a fleeting moment of peak performance but rather a steady state of mind that can be sustained regardless of conditions or circumstances. In other words, composure is a proactive mindset cultivated through deliberate practice and self-awareness. It involves an ongoing radical and visceral acceptance of positive and negative experiences without being swayed by them. Unlike "the zone," which may come and go unpredictably, composure is a quality that traders can develop and strengthen over time, providing a solid foundation for consistent decision-making and performance in the market. Moreover, while "the zone" often implies a narrow focus on the task at hand, composure encompasses a broader perspective that extends beyond individual trades or moments of trading activity. It involves maintaining clarity, perspective, and emotional stability amidst the ups and downs of life itself. This cultivated mindset enables traders to navigate broader life challenges with resilience and adaptability, creating an overall inner experience that deeply favors success and well-being.

As you can see, trading isn't just about numbers, charts, and strategies. It challenges our emotional resilience and demands unparalleled self-restraint and awareness. It requires that we embrace uncertainty, not just superficially but deeply—soul-deep. Hence, the journey we embark on is more than just about money; it is a voyage of self-discovery, a deep dive into the intricacies of our psyche. This book is an endeavor to guide you through that intricate maze. Countless books have been written on the topic already, so I'm not bringing anything new to the table. What I'm endeavoring to do instead is to deliver the information in a way that is simple, relatable, actionable, and perhaps above all, impactful.

Trading is not a get-rich-quick endeavor! It could be, but if you get in for that reason alone, chances are that you will end up disappointed. It is essential to discuss this honestly. Most of the glamorous tales of overnight fortunes you might hear about are outliers, often embellished for the sake of a good story or to sell a particular product or course. While it's true that some traders have achieved rapid success, the majority have had to toil, falter, learn, and persevere over extended periods to realize consistent profitability. One of the primary reasons many aspiring traders find themselves in turbulent waters is that they are inundated with advertisements and stories that paint an overly rosy picture. These tales often gloss over the countless hours of study, the emotional highs and lows, and the sheer persistence required to trade successfully. Instead, they highlight rare windfalls, feeding the fantasy of instant wealth. However, if you peel back the layers and talk to seasoned professionals—real ones, not those in rented Lamborghinis— you'll often hear tales of initial failures, hard-earned lessons, and the painstaking process of refining trading strategies and developing a winning mindset. These narratives provide real educational value, laying bare the complexities and challenges of the trading world, not those from the "trading bros" selling you a get-rich-quick dream.

So why trade if it's not an instant goldmine? Well, beyond the potential for financial gain, trading offers a unique blend of challenges and rewards. It's a continuous learning journey, testing one's analytical skills, emotional resilience, and decision-making abilities under pressure. For many, the thrill lies not just in the profits but in the ability to flow with the chaotic dance of the market and the tremendous opportunities for self-growth this presents. Trading with an appropriate mindset means understanding that it's a marathon, not a sprint. It means cultivating patience, dedicating oneself to continuous learning, and maintaining humility in both wins and losses. It is about the quest for mastery and personal growth as much as it is about the allure of financial rewards.

Drawing from the vast reservoir of my personal trading journey and the privilege of mentoring hundreds of traders over the years, I've discerned a powerful truth: achieving consistency in trading doesn't happen by mere chance or luck. Instead, it hinges on three foundational elements, three cornerstones if you will, that hold the structure of successful trading together. I affectionately refer to these as the "Three Main Pillars of Composure." These pillars are the essence, the guiding principles, which, when deeply understood and integrated, pave the way for a trader's enduring success.

Pillar One: Grasping and Welcoming Uncertainty

The first pillar delves deep into the realm of market uncertainty, a concept that many grapple with, often unknowingly. You see, most traders are blissfully unaware of the inherently chaotic nature of the market. Though they might have an inkling of the uncertainty at play, it's a faint acknowledgment and truly comprehending it remains elusive. At our core, as humans, we are hardwired to seek patterns. We crave predictability—we are creatures of habit and comfort; hence, we are innately designed to resist uncertainty. We yearn for control, for the assurance that if we follow X, Y will undoubtedly follow. However, confronting uncertainty unsettles our deep-seated need for predictability, rendering things inherently challenging psychologically. Instead of facing this uncomfortable truth—the truth of uncertainty—head-on, most traders immerse themselves further into the labyrinth of chart analyses. They subconsciously mold these analyses to fit their biases, sometimes bending reality to a point where they can't discern fact from fantasy. The mental contortions they subject themselves to can be astounding. And when the unforgiving markets shatter these carefully constructed illusions, the fallout is profound. They don't just lose financially; they are emotionally and mentally devastated, having tied their self-worth, aspirations, and very identity to these predictions.

Our brains, fascinatingly complex and evolved, are pattern-seeking devices. From our earliest days as nomadic tribes, our survival depended on our ability to anticipate danger, understand seasonal shifts, and foresee potential food sources. In essence, we are hardwired to resist the unknown because, historically, what we didn't know could harm us. However, this evolutionary trait, so crucial in our past, is a hindrance in the intricate dance of modern trading. In the market, every transaction, every buy or sell order, plunges us into a realm of probabilities, not certainties. Every decision carries a risk, and every prediction has a potential for error. For many traders, especially those just embarking on this journey, this inherent unpredictability often becomes an overwhelming force. The markets don't just test our analytical skills; they challenge our very psychological makeup; hence, most traders respond impulsively when faced with this uncertainty. I am not making a "good or bad" judgment; the fact is that people are simply enacting what they are wired to do via millions of years of evolution. They also perpetually seek solace in so-called "foolproof" strategies. They labor under the illusion that they'll conquer the uncertainty if they can just amass enough data, uncover the right technique, or decipher the ideal pattern. However, more often than not, this quest only amplifies their anxiety. Every unexpected market movement, every unforeseen dip or surge, becomes a source of doubt and stress, leading to rushed decisions, missed opportunities, or ill-timed exits.

True mastery in trading requires a profound shift in mindset. Instead of resisting uncertainty, we must understand, accept, and embrace it. I would even add that we must learn to love it! Rather than viewing uncertainty as an adversary, we should recognize it as a constant companion, a force to be respected but not feared. By truly internalizing this and making peace with the unpredictability, traders can cultivate a calm detachment. From this centered space, decisions are made not from a place of fear or greed but from rational analysis and seasoned intuition. The journey to this enlightened state of trading can be challenging. It demands introspection, self-awareness, and, above all, relentless practice. However, by recognizing our intolerance of uncertainty and by actively working on improving it, we lay the foundation for not just trading success but a more balanced, harmonious approach to the myriad uncertainties of life itself. Hence, this first pillar is pivotal; its significance cannot be overstated.

Pillar Two: Fostering a Resilient Emotional Core

Diving deep into the world of uncertainty, after dissecting its various facets and reshaping your perception of it, leads you to the next challenging frontier: mastering the internal storms that such uncertainty unleashes. This journey demands introspection. And a lot of it! It's a call to look inward, to scrutinize the intricate whirls of your thoughts, your emotions, and the very fabric of your identity. The goal of this journey is to develop emotional equilibrium, an anchor that steadies you amid the volatility of markets. Imagine navigating the tumultuous seas of trading without such an anchor. You would agree, it's not recommendable. Market movements are bound to send your heart racing and your emotions spiraling. The wear and tear on your psyche won't make trading sustainable.

Understand this: consistent profitability in trading doesn't hinge solely on market acumen. This can't be said enough. Consistent profitability also leans (heavily) on one's ability to stay grounded when faced with market uncertainty. You cannot succeed as a trader if you don't understand this. It's not my intention to paint a grim picture but rather to emphasize the absolute necessity of emotional discipline in this profession. Visualize a sniper stationed with a singular objective, waiting for that perfect shot. The sniper's prowess isn't just in their skill but in their ability to remain calm, patient, and focused. Similarly, as a trader, if your elation soars with every win, if despair plummets with each loss, not only will you lose sight of your objective, but the emotional toll will lead to reckless decisions, jeopardizing your trading journey. The bedrock of enduring success in trading lies in cultivating unwavering emotional stability amidst the inevitable storms of the market. Hence, this second pillar is another pivot in achieving the behavioral consistency needed to sustain profitability. Rest assured, developing emotional stability isn't a herculean task; however, it does require commitment.

In the pursuit of regulating one's emotions, meditation presents itself as one of the most potent tools. Meditation is not just a practice; it's an exploration, a journey inward. It offers us a mirror to our innermost thoughts and emotions, allowing us to become acquainted with the transient nature of our thoughts and feelings. As traders, the market constantly challenges our composure, pulling at the strings of our patience and resilience. Meditation teaches us to observe these internal fluctuations without becoming entangled in them. Just as a bodybuilder trains at the gym to enhance physical strength and mass, meditators use meditation to bolster their mental muscles, fortifying qualities like patience, resilience, and composure. The financial titans of Wall Street, including luminaries like Paul Tudor Jones, Ray Dalio, and Daniel Loeb, have all recognized and harnessed the unparalleled advantages of meditation. Their endorsement of this ancient practice in modern high-stakes trading is a testament to its efficacy (Baer 2014). In an arena where every decision carries weight, these magnates have found solace and clarity in the stillness of meditation. In fact, the embrace of meditation has become so widespread in the financial world that renowned firms like Goldman Sachs now offer meditation classes and seminars, with waiting lists stretching into the hundreds, as reported by Bloomberg (Burton and Effinger 2014). That is because meditation works! It isn't just another trending buzzword; it's a transformative, scientifically backed approach that empowers you to adopt a researcher's lens, delving deeply into the intricacies of your psyche and understanding its ebbs and flows. As a result, clarity, focus, and composure are all improved.

Drawing from my intensive forays into meditation during intensive months-long retreats and everyday life, I can vouch for its transformative potential. The richness and depth it has brought to my perception, understanding, and management of my inner world are unparalleled. On a foundational level, it has illuminated the inner workings of my psyche. It has shed light on the intricate dance of emotions, impulses, and thoughts, allowing for more mindful responses, especially in high-pressure situations typical in trading. The ramifications of such heightened self-awareness regarding my trading psychology were profound. Having said that, tempering expectations is crucial. While meditation is, indeed, powerful, it's not a magical elixir that remedies all challenges. It doesn't erase problems but equips you to navigate them with greater resilience and clarity. Additionally, meditation is a journey, not a destination. It demands dedication, persistence, and unwavering commitment. However, for those willing to embark on this path, the rewards—in trading and life—are truly immeasurable.

Pillar Three: The Accountability Factor

In the vast expanse of information on trading, much of what you'll stumble upon is steeped in theory—to some extent, so are the insights found within the pages of this book. Theory is foundational as it sketches out the path; however, the transformative journey comes alive in the act of walking that path—through relentless implementation, hands-on practice, and unwavering dedication to the craft. And the final beacon guiding this journey? Accountability. After having developed a proper understanding of uncertainty (pillar one), as you keep working on the emotional management component (pillar two), accountability is the last piece of the behavioral consistency puzzle—it will make a world of difference to your bottom line.

For instance, take the story of the billionaire trader and hedge fund titan Paul Tudor Jones. In his quest for unwavering discipline and focus, he sought counsel from Tony Robbins, the celebrated motivational guru. The value Tudor Jones placed on this advisory relationship was evident in the substantial fees, running into millions, that he willingly disbursed. As reported by *Business Insider* (Feloni 2017), this relationship profoundly impacted Jones's trading trajectory. Robbins became pivotal in anchoring Tudor Jones during his trading endeavors, holding him accountable at every turn. Furthermore, at another juncture, the illustrious Deepak Chopra also played a guiding role for Jones.

Consider the emphasis on accountability for a seasoned expert like Tudor Jones. The truth is that self-accountability is one of the most elusive disciplines for most of us. This statement isn't just about trading; it's about life. Whether it's sticking to a rigorous diet, keeping up with fitness goals, or resisting the urge to light up another cigarette, we constantly grapple with our commitments.

Even our most iron-clad resolutions can waver in the face of shifting moods and fleeting desires. Willpower, as powerful as it can be, is also temperamental, wearing thin amidst daily challenges. Relying solely on it is a gamble. That's where the strength of external accountability steps in, acting as a steadfast lighthouse guiding us back when we drift off course. Such external accountability doesn't diminish our capabilities or self-worth; rather, it magnifies our potential. It's akin to having a co-pilot on a treacherous journey, ensuring we don't lose our way. When we openly commit to someone else—a mentor, a coach, or even a dedicated peer group—we are not just voicing our goals; we are solidifying our dedication to achieving them. It becomes a symbiotic relationship where growth, consistency, and progress are the fruits reaped. Hence, if the likes of Tudor Jones, with all their expertise and prowess, see the merit in external accountability, it underscores its pivotal role in success. Whether in trading or any endeavor, weaving in this support can be the transformative element that elevates one from good to exceptional.

In this book, we'll embark on a deep exploration of these three foundational pillars that form the bedrock of trading consistency. These pillars represent not just a method but also the most direct route to enduring profitability in trading. I state this with conviction, drawing from my extensive years fine-tuning my own trading psyche. I've broken down the key elements of my success in the market, pinpointing fundamental principles that have also propelled many others. This is how this three-pillar approach was born. Over the years, I've meticulously honed it, guiding numerous traders to the pinnacle of their potential.

I have grappled with the same challenges you might currently face in your trading; I've sifted through the overwhelming inundation of information, most of which can be misleading or irrelevant. The market is rife with those who gamble under the guise of trading, and it's a travesty that earnest individuals get ensnared in such traps. With utmost sincerity, I wish to shepherd you through this maze. Believe me when I say my commitment to your success is personal. With a profound grasp of these pillars and a relentless pursuit to embody them, you will not only differentiate yourself from the herd but also massively improve your luck in the market, catapulting yourself into the echelons of trading elites.

This three-pillar approach is logical, pragmatic, time-tested, and scientific. But above all, it's easy to grasp and implement. The typical trading psychology book is very dense. It covers a lot of ground and is often entrenched in academic rhetoric. These pieces of work are helpful, but they are often removed from the realities of trading. They are written by those who have never felt the pulse of live markets. I present a contrast. My foundation may not be based on ornate academic degrees, but it is solidified by hands-on experience. A lot of it! Thousands of trades, countless traders coached to success, and an intrinsic understanding of what truly constitutes a winning trading psychology—this is the perspective I offer.

Let me emphasize: simplicity is strength. I aim to demystify, not complicate. There is beauty in stripping things down to their core, eschewing unnecessary complexities. Adding verbose explanations or grandiose lexicon only muddies the waters. Instead, I've chosen clarity and simplicity as my allies, hoping to make the voyage ahead smoother and more enlightening for you. As you delve deeper into this book, I invite you to approach it not just as a manual but as a companion on your journey to mastering the intricate dance of the market. Ground yourself in the three pillars mentioned above. Doing so will instantaneously elevate your game, distinguishing you from the multitude. Once you've cemented this foundation, you can venture—if you want—into more complex trading psychology topics to further hone your mental edge.

In closing this segment, it's worth noting that readers may hold differing opinions or perspectives, and that is perfectly fine. However, I earnestly request that you approach this work with an open heart and mind. The wisdom encapsulated here isn't merely a product of fleeting trends but stands as an enduring beacon. If you allow yourself even a modicum of openness, you'll recognize that the principles in these pages transcend trading, reflecting deeper truths about the art of living itself.

Chapter 2
Pillar One: Grasping and Welcoming Uncertainty

Uncertainty: The Name of the Game

At the core of my beliefs lies the principle that nothing is conclusively certain. This ethos of probabilistic thinking or reasoning has been the compass for my life for years now, both inside and outside the trading world. Embracing probabilistic thinking isn't just a theoretical framework for me; it is a deeply ingrained habit and discipline that has become an integral part of my mental fabric. This mindset was cultivated and crystallized through my extensive experiences in trading, reinforced by the sheer volume of trades I've executed and the countless hours I've spent engaging with the market. A pivotal aspect of this mindset is my demeanor toward the market. While none of us is without ego, several investors in my fund who have had the privilege to watch me trade often comment on the striking absence of ego in my trading decisions. According to them, my interactions with the market seem remarkably devoid of emotional biases. Of course, this isn't always true—I'm not a robot or a brain-dead zombie—but it generally is. However, it wasn't always like that, as the journey I shared in the first chapter reveals.

From an early age, I knew that I was going to have a life as a risk manager. I always felt the pull to understand and control the uncertainties in my life, and it was this magnetic pull that led me to the narrative of Darvas. Beneath the glimmer of wealth lay a deep-rooted desire to break free from the incessant chaos of my life. Growing up with a mentally unstable parent, I rarely had the luxury of certainty and predictability. Every day brought adversity, shame, pain—things could go sour in the blink of an eye. Hence, for me, trading wasn't merely about making money; it was a journey of harnessing my potential and carving an alternative route for my future. As a kid, I recall being engrossed in games of Monopoly with my cousins or siblings. During each game, I meticulously calculated the odds, weighing the benefits against the risks. I reveled in the challenge of predicting outcomes. In many ways, this innate urge to control the unknown guided me toward the financial world, where risk, reward, and chaos played out on a grand stage. However, this innate affinity for strategic thinking, risk assessment, and predicting outcomes lacked a crucial element: a deep acceptance of uncertainty.

All my life, I inadvertently nurtured an aversion to what is unpredictable. And when I entered the trading arena, the market, with its ever-fluctuating nature, presented the ultimate test for me. It was a humbling experience to acknowledge that no amount of strategic planning could account for every eventuality. As I kept engaging with the market over the years, it became clear that true mastery isn't necessarily about predicting outcomes but embracing the unpredictable. It is about learning to dance with uncertainty, to see it not as an adversary but as an essential partner in the intricate ballet of trading. While I had always been on a quest to control and foresee, the market, through its stern lessons, taught me the value of acceptance. Accepting uncertainty doesn't mean relinquishing control; it means recalibrating your approach and finding harmony in the ebb and flow. It's about realizing that the journey of trading, much like life itself, is less about rigid predictions and more about navigating the undulating waves with grace, resilience, and an open heart.

I've worked with a lot of traders in my coaching practice, many of whom possess intellectual prowess that far surpasses my own. Yet, I've observed a pattern that hindered their progress: they were ensnared in what I call the "prediction paradigm." Despite their keen analytical minds, they hadn't truly grappled with the intrinsic uncertainty of the market. They sidestepped the introspective journey needed to not only accept this uncertainty but also embrace it. While their cerebral capabilities were undeniably impressive, this singular focus on prediction impeded their consistency in trading. Their journey through the financial markets was akin to a tumultuous ride, with the highs and lows of their trades directly influencing their emotional states. Successful trades sent them soaring to euphoric heights while losing ones plunged them into the depths of despair. This emotional volatility, in turn, clouded their judgment and exacerbated the cycle. The absence of a well-calibrated trading psychology is all too common and reflects the reality for most traders.

Consistent success in trading is not solely a product of intellect; it's the marriage of cognitive skill with emotional stability and a profound understanding of the market's chaotic nature. For many, breaking free from the shackles of the prediction paradigm requires a paradigm shift, a recalibration of their understanding of the market, and a deeper dive into understanding themselves. This work is imperative since an inability to comfortably coexist with the uncertain nature of markets will inevitably give rise to a plethora of behavioral pitfalls and miscalculations.

For instance:

1. **Compulsive Trading:** Often, traders find themselves unsettled by the mere idea of not having an active stake in the market. This discomfort, intensified by the apprehension of missing out on potential profits, propels them to undertake trades without rigorous adherence to their predetermined strategies or thorough analysis. Such rash decisions invariably tilt the scale toward losses.

2. **Adjusting Stop-Losses Arbitrarily:** With a stop-loss set to curtail potential damages, uncertainty-fueled dread often emerges as the market edges closer to this threshold. The reluctance to acknowledge and accept a loss tempts traders to shift the stop further, clinging to the optimism of a market reversal. Regrettably, this often amplifies the damage.

3. **Indecision:** Even when a golden opportunity, perfectly aligning with a trader's criteria, presents itself, the shadows of doubt and the phobia of incurring a loss can cause paralysis. This hesitation can rob them of a potentially lucrative trade.

4. **Doubling Down on a Declining Position:** When faced with the discomfort of a losing position, a trader's aversion to being wrong may spur them to double down on that losing position, banking on a market turnaround. Often, this only deepens their financial pit.

5. **Premature Exits:** The specter of uncertainty can push traders into second-guessing their meticulously crafted strategies. They might hastily abandon a position, dreading a potential downturn, only to witness the market persisting in the very direction they had anticipated.

6. **Overlooking Risk Management:** Entrapped by price patterns that appear predictable, a trader might recklessly stake an unreasonable chunk of their funds on a singular trade, lured by the allure of a massive win. This endangers the stability of their entire financial portfolio.

7. **Chasing the Market:** Having missed an initial surge, traders, fueled by the dread of losing out on subsequent opportunities, might hastily enter, often at an unfavorable juncture. This typically culminates in entering either at a pinnacle or a nadir, swiftly followed by an immediate market reversal.

8. **Succumbing to Confirmation Bias:** There's a tendency, especially when confronted with uncertainty, to seek validation. Traders may lean toward analyses that confirm and affirm their existing stance, conveniently ignoring contradictory signals. This blinkered approach jeopardizes objective analysis and paves the way for erroneous judgments and decision-making.

These trading pitfalls, diverse as they may seem, all trace back to an overarching struggle: the human resistance to market uncertainty. Recognizing this core challenge and actively working to overcome it can empower traders with enhanced strategies and a mindset more conducive to success. By prioritizing understanding, acceptance, and a measured approach to uncertainty, traders can better insulate themselves against these common missteps and cultivate a more harmonious relationship with the market.

Unpacking Uncertainty

Before we go any further, let me define what I understand by the term "uncertainty." Given that it's a term that can be viewed through various lenses, I want to lay out my perspective to ensure we're on the same page. At its core, uncertainty refers to situations where the future remains ambiguous. It signifies moments when, despite our best efforts, we lack the complete information to accurately forecast the future. We are working with fragments of information, trying to piece together a coherent picture, but there exist gaps in our knowledge.

Now, closely intertwined with uncertainty is its practical counterpart: risk. While uncertainty revolves around our cognitive grasp of the future, risk pertains to the tangible stakes involved. It's what is on the line due to the unpredictable scenarios we face. Picture this: You're a trader betting that a particular stock will rise. You set a stop-loss just below a crucial support level, with a potential risk of $1. In line with its uncertain nature, the market takes a turn you didn't anticipate, hitting your stop. You are now a dollar short. Here, your tangible loss of a dollar was the "risk" you took, which arose from the inherent "uncertainty" of market movements. It bears emphasizing: Although we can quantify risk and set our thresholds for acceptable losses, pinning down uncertainty with exactitude proves to be more elusive. This inherent unpredictability is precisely what defines the concept of "uncertainty." The term "uncertainty" originates from the Latin word *incertum* or *incertus*. It is composed of the prefix *in-*, which implies negation, and *certum* or *certus*, which means "certain" or "settled." Thus, *incertum* or *incertus* conveys a sense of ambiguity, doubt, or lack of clarity or definitiveness about something.

What fuels the presence of uncertainty? Once again, the issue's essence lies in the limitations of our knowledge. It's primarily because our predictions are made with incomplete information about the countless factors influencing one another. This absence of comprehensive knowledge stems from the sheer complexity of the world around us. An innumerable number of factors, some overt and others subtle, collectively influence outcomes. Each of these variables, from environmental conditions to individual decision-making processes and even unforeseen events, plays a part in shaping the final result. But remember, it's not just the market that is shrouded in uncertainty. Life itself teems with it, often hiding in plain sight. Consider the weather: It remains one of the most unpredictable facets of our lives. Even with state-of-the-art forecasting technologies, meteorologists frequently find themselves on the wrong foot, showcasing the capricious nature of the weather. Or contemplate health: No matter the lengths we go to in maintaining a healthy lifestyle, the future of our health remains uncertain. We might adopt the best preventive measures, but there's never a foolproof shield against ailments or injuries. Relationships offer another lens: They remain one of the most intricate dances of human experience. Even the most steadfast bonds, built over years, aren't immune to change. Humans evolve, situations shift, and the dynamics of relationships can morph, sometimes catching us off guard and bringing both pleasant and challenging surprises.

Every facet of our existence, from our career trajectories to personal discoveries, is punctuated with moments of uncertainty. It's this omnipresent uncertainty that makes life simultaneously thrilling, challenging, and profound. A crucial takeaway is that uncertainty exists on a spectrum. At one extreme, you encounter events that defy prediction. In contrast, at the opposite end, you find events characterized by an exceptionally high degree of predictability, often referred to as scientific uncertainty. Between these two extremes lie myriad scenarios with varying degrees of predictability.

Take, for instance, the daily phenomenon of the sun rising. While it seems absolute certainty that we will witness a sunrise every day, it is not entirely guaranteed. Given our knowledge of astronomy and the consistent patterns we've observed over millennia, we can conclude that the probability of the sun rising tomorrow is exceptionally high—a scientific certainty. Relying on this with a high degree of certainty makes logical sense, given the overwhelming evidence supporting this outcome.

Another example is health risks influenced by geography and environment. If you're residing in the United States, the odds of succumbing to malaria are virtually negligible, thanks to advanced healthcare and a climate less conducive to the disease. However, shift your location to certain parts of Africa, especially regions grappling with the disease, and the odds change dramatically. Your probability of contracting Malaria rises simply based on geographic location.

Providing another lens is natural disasters. Residents of California might be well acquainted with the possibility of earthquakes due to its location along the Pacific Ring of Fire. Conversely, people living in the Midwest might be more attuned to the threats of tornadoes. Understanding the specific risks associated with one's geographic location can help one make better choices, from housing to insurance purchases.

Consider next the allure of lottery jackpots. The tantalizing idea of winning life-changing sums of money with a mere ticket often blinds us to the stark probabilities. For Mega Millions, you are more likely to get struck by lightning or die in a plane crash than to hit the jackpot (More 2022). Holding onto the belief that you'll someday win against such staggering odds might not be the most practical use of hope or expectation.

Speaking of plane crashes, the number of flights that traverse the globe daily without incident is staggering. While plane crashes, when they do occur, garner significant media attention, they are statistical anomalies. The overwhelming majority of flights take off and land safely, making air travel one of the safest modes of transportation. Yet, the fear of flying persists in many, often overshadowing the high probability of safety.

One last example—something closer to home. Suppose you have been to a particular restaurant multiple times. You know the menu, appreciate the ambiance, and believe the quality of food and service are top-notch. Going here is akin to the certainty of the sun rising every day. It's a highly predictable experience—you know you can expect a good meal. However, let's say you are exploring a new city and randomly walk into a restaurant with no prior knowledge, no reviews, no recommendations. Here, the uncertainty is highest. You are essentially rolling the dice on the experience. The outcome could be delightful or disappointing, and you are basing your decision on spontaneity and adventure.

The crux of the matter is this: there is no absolute certainty. We often ascribe a sense of certainty to some events, not because they are truly devoid of uncertainty, but rather for the sake of practicality and convenience. However, it's vital to acknowledge that, in reality, uncertainty is an ever-present companion on our journey through life. This acknowledgment of the omnipresence of uncertainty necessitates an invaluable virtue: humility. Humility becomes our grounding anchor in the face of the vast unknowns that envelop our daily existence. It reminds us that no matter how knowledgeable, skilled, or experienced we become, there will always be elements outside our control and understanding. We'll revisit the concept of humility later in this chapter.

Uncertainty in the Market

Markets have a lot of short-term uncertainty, perhaps more than most people realize or are willing to admit. At the heart of market dynamics lies a straightforward yet profound principle: every fluctuation in price, whether slight or substantial, derives from market participants' expectations about future outcomes. To reiterate, the entire dance of numbers that we observe on market charts—every uptick or downtick—is, at its core, a manifestation of collective expectations about what lies ahead. This principle is so central that understanding it is crucial for anyone looking to decode the mysteries of financial markets.

Let's distill this intricate mechanism into a more relatable scenario. Imagine you are in a cozy room with nine other people, and in your possession is an alluring painting that has piqued the interest of the others. The dynamics of this room closely mimic a market, where the people represent participants, and the goods or services they're interested in trading are represented by the painting. Suppose you've tagged your painting at a value of $200. Another person, deeply captivated by the artwork, offers you $210. But what prompts this individual to propose a higher price than the sticker amount? Well, the answer is rooted in their expectations of the future. By offering $210, the buyer is signaling their belief that the painting's value will escalate beyond the current price. They anticipate that either the demand for the painting will rise or some external factor will amplify its worth. This is a speculation, a bet on the future (see Figure 2.1).

The sale culminates at $210. Fast-forward, the same buyer now intends to resell the painting. He pitches a price of $220 but finds no takers. However, after gauging the situation, an observant individual in the room considers $215 a justifiable amount and offers to buy it at that price. Again, beneath this offer lies a conjecture about the future. In offering a price lower than the asking rate, the buyer is signaling a lower level of confidence in the artwork's potential appreciation. The seller agrees to the transaction, securing a $5 profit—after all, profit is profit (see Figure 2.2).

In a dramatic twist, the room buzzes with whispers that the painting is the work of a renowned artist. Its perceived value skyrockets within seconds. Bidding wars ensue, and in a whirlwind of transactions, the painting lands a price tag of $600. Such is the volatility infused by information and sentiment in our hypothetical market (see Figure 2.3).

Later, doubts creep in; the high-roller who splurged $600 on the painting grapples with buyer's remorse. The demand dips, and he's forced to reconsider his asking price, settling at $425, reflecting the shifting sentiment in the room (see Figure 2.4).

Does this seem familiar? It should be because this ebb and flow of prices based on collective beliefs and speculations, scaled up millions of times, is precisely how global markets operate. Replace the

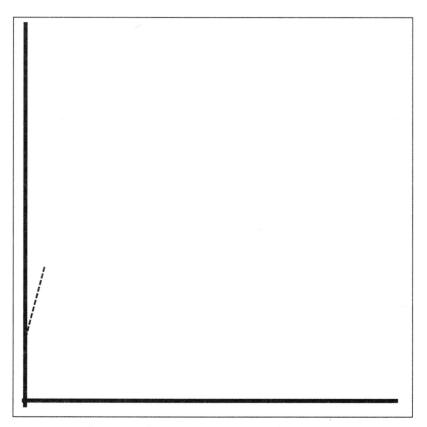

Figure 2.1 An illustration that captures a moment when a desired painting surges in price because of its perceived value.

room with the world, the 10 participants with millions of them, and the painting with stocks, commodities, forex, or cryptocurrencies, and you have the intricate tapestry of financial markets.

Every "tick"—the most minor change in price for a traded instrument—is the market's heartbeat. It encapsulates the consensus at that fleeting moment, representing the aggregate of all buying and selling pressures. An "uptick" transpires when the aggregated weight of buying exceeds selling. This means that traders are ready to pay more than the last listed price. But what drives them to this stance? It boils down to their perception of the future.

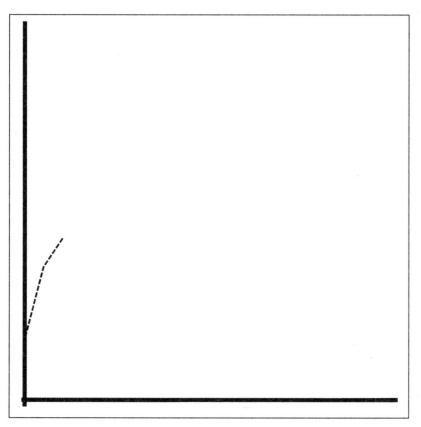

Figure 2.2   The buyer, now turned seller, navigates offers and counteroffers, ultimately leading to a modest profit in the face of shifting confidence.

If they are of the conviction that the current price is undervalued in comparison to its potential future value, they are inclined to buy at a rate higher than the previous transaction. This act of buying at a steeper price propels the overall price upwards. Contrastingly, a "downtick" emerges when selling pressure outweighs buying. In this scenario, traders are inclined to pitch prices below the most recent transaction rate. This behavior stems from the belief that the current price is inflated, forecasting a potential dip in the future. Thus, they quote lower prices, which, when transacted, drive the price downwards.

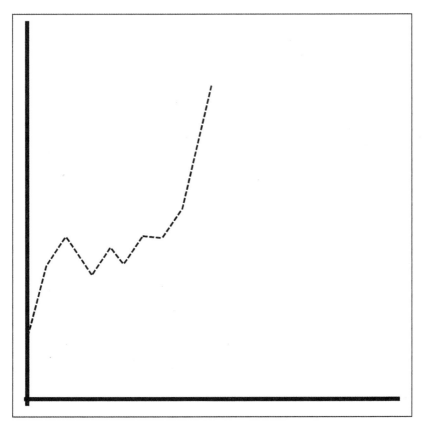

Figure 2.3   When new information ignites a frenzy of bids, catapulting the painting's value to unprecedented heights.

To simplify further, the direction of price movement is predominantly a function of the collective's willingness to pay. This willingness is, in turn, anchored in expectations. These expectations are formed by an amalgam of factors—from hard data like news and fundamentals to softer variables like individual aspirations, emotions, and market psychology. Each tick, whether upwards or downwards, gradually builds the larger picture we recognize as minute, hourly, daily, or weekly candlestick patterns on charts. Fundamentally, these movements reflect the constant tug-of-war between two predominant sentiments—optimism and pessimism—as they relate to

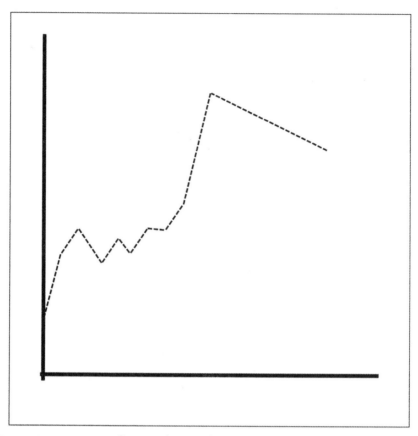

Figure 2.4 In a turn of events, the once-high-priced painting faces a downturn, embodying the fickle nature of sentiment and its consequences.

the future. Prices tend to gravitate within a narrow band when these forces are balanced. This is a period characterized by reduced volatility, where neither sentiment has the upper hand (see Figure 2.5).

However, price directions become more pronounced when one sentiment significantly overpowers the other. This could manifest as either an uptrend, driven by dominant optimism, or a downtrend, propelled by prevailing pessimism (see Figure 2.6).

Ultimately, the magnitude and duration of these market movements lie in participants' convictions. To reiterate, those with a firm

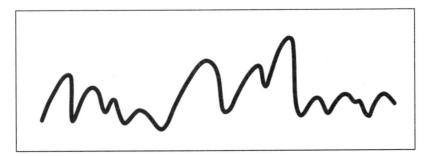

Figure 2.5　This depiction represents a period of rangebound activity, where neither optimism nor pessimism has the upper hand.

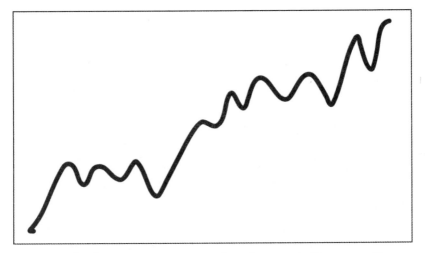

Figure 2.6　This depiction captures a trending phase marked by a prevailing sense of optimism.

expectation about the future, demonstrated by their purchasing or selling actions, often dictate the direction. An accumulated positive sentiment leads to rising trends, while an aggregated negative sentiment prompts downtrends. When neither sentiment holds significant sway, the market moves sideways, signifying volatility contraction. This dance, ceaseless and dynamic, is the lifeblood of markets, and understanding its nuances is the key to successful trading.

Now, let's go back to the idea of uncertainty. This is a crucial element of the market that stands out like a beacon. This ubiquitous factor is always present, shaping the landscape of market dynamics. Let's focus on its elemental facet—will the next tick be for the buy side, or will it be for the sell side? This is the enigma, the profound uncertainty every trader grapples with. What will happen next? The real, unbiased answer is nobody knows. The myriad influences steering the market at any given second are too overwhelming. Every market participant carries with them unique interests, beliefs, biases, expectations, motivations, and varying degrees of financial clout. Trying to pinpoint, with unwavering confidence, how these multifaceted forces collectively steer market direction is like attempting to predict the exact pattern of falling leaves on a windy day. And the lower the time frame, the truer this is. It's like navigating a storm, where news and rumors serve as lightning strikes, capable of causing swift, dramatic price alterations. Occasionally, these tumultuous movements ripple into larger trends on the higher time frame, but more often than not, they're fleeting, mere emotional blips that don't necessarily alter the overarching trend (see Figure 2.7).

News, in the trading realm, is particularly unpredictable. For instance, a groundbreaking announcement makes headlines. How will traders react? Will they plunge into a frenzy of buying, driven by optimism? Will they pull back, gripped by caution or even fear? And sometimes, the markets' response is counterintuitive— uplifting news can lead to a selloff, while grim updates might catalyze a buying spree. Such paradoxes are commonplace, reinforcing the notion of uncertainty. One must also consider the vast array of motivations propelling traders to act. An individual might decide to offload a stock, not due to market indicators but merely to fund a dream vacation or a home upgrade. Such a move, especially if it's substantial, could inadvertently shake the market, affecting countless other trades in the process, generating a ripple effect that is hard to quantify. Consider a real-world scenario: You have done your research, have crunched the numbers, and your strategy indicates an opportune moment to go short. Yet, another trader,

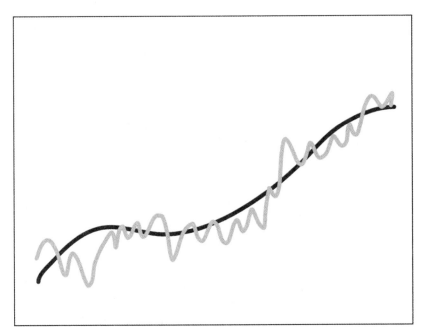

Figure 2.7   This figure encapsulates the chaotic nature of short-term price fluctuations and their often ephemeral impact on the overall market trajectory.

analyzing the exact same data, might opt to go long. If their conviction translates into a sizable purchase, the market could pivot, potentially thwarting your trade. It all circles back to the basic economic principle: When demand overshadows supply, prices climb; inversely, when supply swamps demand, a dip ensues.

Moreover, human nature is inherently predisposed toward emulation and mirroring the actions of others. Buying pressure might inspire a cascade of additional buying activity, amplifying the upward trajectory. Conversely, selling pressure might inspire a cascade of additional selling activity, amplifying the downward trajectory. However, the operative term here is "might." The market's reaction is not always uniform or guaranteed. At times, the anticipated cascade might not materialize, and occasionally, the market may even respond contrarily. Predicting these nuances with precision is a challenging feat.

Time Frame's Impact on Predictability

The time frame of the chart being analyzed significantly impacts predictability. One of the factors making broader time frames, such as weekly and monthly charts, more predictable is the extended progression of time. These lengthier durations tend to showcase cyclical patterns that reflect overarching global macroeconomic trends, which, for the most part, are somewhat foreseeable. On the flip side, when we zero in on shorter periods, particularly intraday periods, the clarity diminishes. The ebb and flow of individual actions and decisions create a cacophony, making these time frames inherently noisier (see Figure 2.8).

Consider major events like the tech boom of the late 1990s, the financial crisis of 2008, or even the more recent pandemic-induced economic changes. While they had daily fluctuations and volatility, their real gravity and sustained impact were best observed on broader chart time frames. It's akin to viewing a landscape from a higher vantage point—the daily details and imperfections get smoothed out, and one can see the larger patterns and formations taking shape. This is not to say that these extended time frames are

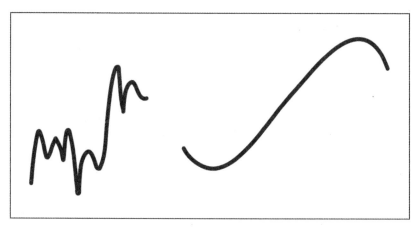

Figure 2.8   Short-term vs. long-term—this figure explores how time frames can impact predictability.

devoid of uncertainty. They, too, have their share of unpredictabili-
ties, but the nature of this uncertainty is different. Instead of reacting to immediate stimuli, these charts respond to the gradual shifts
in economic tides and prolonged market sentiments. This is why
many long-term investors and institutional traders place significant
weight on these time frames, as they provide a clearer, more holistic
view of the market's direction.

It is crucial to understand that this doesn't imply markets
inherently behave differently across varying time frames. Indeed,
markets are fractal in nature—in other words, the patterns observed
are self-similar, no matter how much you zoom in or out. Hence,
strip away the dimension of time, and the essence of price movements, patterns, and formations remains consistent across the
board. The real issue at hand, especially with shorter time frames,
is, again, the accelerated feedback loop. This swift feedback can
lead traders to make ill-advised, impulsive decisions. Our cognitive
wiring isn't necessarily attuned to making clear-headed choices
when faced with rapid feedback, leading to potential trading blun-
ders. In the heat of the moment, one might cling to a plummeting
stock or hastily sell a rising one. The allure of immediate gains or
the sting of quick losses can distort judgment. In contrast, broader
time frames afford traders the luxury of time, allowing for more
deliberate decision-making. The slower feedback inherent in these
higher time frames fosters a more rational approach, free from the
frenzy of moment-to-moment fluctuations.

Acknowledging the greater uncertainty inherent to short-term
time frames doesn't imply an inevitable defeat for short-term traders. Quite the contrary! With the right approach and mindset, short-
term trading can be viable and immensely rewarding. Success in
those lower time frames demands heightened precision and systematic rigor. Here, there's little room for indecision or whimsical
shifts in strategy. Markets, in their chaotic dances, are unforgiving
of hesitation or inconsistency. It's like venturing into a tempestuous
sea; without a sturdy, well-navigated ship, you're at the mercy of the
waves. As such, short-term trading mandates a robust framework,

particularly in risk management. The stakes are higher, the margins slimmer, and the room for error is drastically reduced. If you allow doubt to creep into your trading decisions and permit emotion-driven behaviors, the market will invariably capitalize on these vulnerabilities. In other words, if you engage haphazardly with the market over the shorter time frames, the outcomes will inevitably mirror that randomness. However, this should not discourage; rather, it should serve as a clarion call for discipline and consistency. Embodying this principle is crucial: consistency begets consistency. By staying steadfast, relying on a tried-and-tested process, and executing with unwavering consistency, you can and will prevail. In a realm of greater uncertainty, your consistency becomes the stabilizing force; it acts as your North Star, guiding you through the tumultuous waves and ensuring you remain on course.

The Predictive Value of Price Patterns and Formations

Let's indulge in a thought experiment. Consider the chart in Figure 2.9 and ponder its source for a moment.

Now, allow me to clarify: The chart showcases the outcomes of 500 coin flips, all meticulously simulated through a specialized Excel spreadsheet. I created this spreadsheet to generate random results, mirroring the unpredictable nature of actual coin tosses. This apparently simple record of random events bears a striking resemblance to the ebb and flow witnessed in dynamically evolving systems like markets. A technical analyst, when faced with this chart devoid of context, might discern familiar technical patterns such as an "ascending triangle," a "double bottom," or even a "head and shoulders." The assumption would be that these patterns indicate a predictable future movement. However, the inherent catch is straightforward: this chart is birthed from pure randomness; a fair coin was flipped 500 times, and the results—patterns of heads and tails—were recorded (see Figure 2.10).

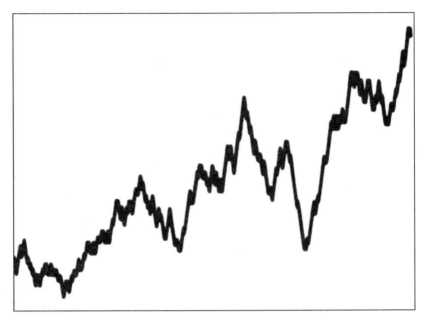

Figure 2.9 Examine the graphic and ponder its potential trajectory.

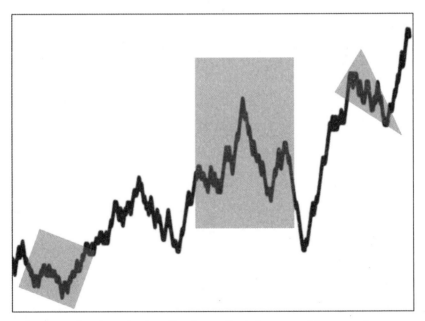

Figure 2.10 This chart displays familiar technical patterns like "ascending triangle," "double bottom," or "head and shoulders," yet its foundation rests on randomness.

This simple experiment should prompt introspection into the fabric of our understanding of the market. Price patterns, often touted as insights into the very nature of what moves the market, might seem tempting to abide by. Yet, there is no tangible metric to gauge how many market players bank on these patterns as opposed to those who regard them as mere noise. This brings us squarely back to our central theme: the omnipresence of uncertainty. Sequences, patterns, and streaks aren't aberrations but statistical norms and don't necessarily hold any predictive value.

Here are some other ubiquitous instances of random sequences that, when graphed, manifest discernable patterns, trajectories, or trends:

- Meteorological Shifts: Day-to-day weather fluctuations.
- Road Traffic: The influx of vehicles at a crossroad over a duration.
- Casino Games: Each slot machine spin.
- Disease Proliferation: The transmission patterns of illnesses within populations.
- Radioactive Disintegration: The spontaneity of atomic decay.
- Board Games: The outcome of dice throws in games like Monopoly.
- Music Playlists: The sequence in which shuffled playlists present songs.
- Wildlife Activities: Actions like a bird's flight or ant trails.
- Social Media Algorithms: The way content appears on user feeds.
- Athletic Competitions: The outcomes in evenly matched sports encounters.
- Emotional Shifts: Mood variations in individuals based on myriad factors.
- Nature Encounters: The species or occurrences one might witness on excursions.
- Dream Sequences: The erratic nature of dreams and their narratives.
- Cloud Patterns: The formation and morphology of clouds on any given day.

I could go on and on. Though swayed by specific influences, each of these processes bears a core of unpredictability. While patterns might emerge, they're often based on probabilities rather than certainties, and again, they don't necessarily have to mean anything. For example, identifying a "head and shoulders" pattern in a chart illustrating an epidemic's spread doesn't necessarily mean that the disease will soon recede and vanish. It's imperative to approach patterns with caution. It's easy to fall into the trap of attributing meaning to patterns simply because they're familiar.

Pivoting to a psychological perspective, our brains, molded by millennia of evolution, naturally seek certainty and gravitate toward recognizing patterns, a critical survival trait. This innate tendency compels us to identify shapes in clouds, anticipate weather changes, or sense the presence of predators. Our cognitive systems continuously strive to decipher patterns and predict future outcomes. However, this evolutionary advantage also has its drawbacks. While our inclination toward pattern detection aids in decision-making, it can also lead us to perceive connections where none exist, potentially skewing our perceptions. This cognitive bias causes us to ascribe specific meanings to random patterns, leading to erroneous conclusions.

Though the market provides opportunities for strategic gains based on observable trends, a discerning trader always remains wary. Ascribing meaning to random patterns can result in detrimental choices. In essence, markets, akin to our vast cosmos, oscillate between structured predictability and randomness. Navigating this intricate maze requires understanding its dual nature and remaining vigilant against our inherent cognitive predispositions. This constant dance between order and chaos isn't exclusive to financial systems but resonates across many phenomena in our universe, from nature's rhythms to celestial dances to even the patterns of our thoughts. The propensity for seeking patterns stems from a deep-rooted inclination within us—a human tendency to seek order in chaos, to find causality amidst the apparent randomness. We instinctively crave to establish connections and predict the future, and in doing that, we give meaning to patterns that might not always have substantive significance.

Now, such a perspective doesn't outright reject the validity of all patterns but instead encourages a balanced and critical approach toward them. Patterns can provide valuable insights, but they're not foolproof indicators of the future. Recognizing a pattern is just the first step; understanding its causative factors, historical context, and limitations is equally vital. Patterns should serve as potential guides, not the gospel. They should be used to inform decisions, not dictate them unequivocally, because they are just one variable within the arsenal of variables that shape the market.

At its heart, trading is an endeavor deeply rooted in pattern analysis; however, each analytical framework has its constraints— from the nuanced assessment of bare price actions to the insights gleaned from order flows, price indicators, and volume metrics. We can analyze and crunch numbers all we want, but we can't wave a magic wand and say, "Hey, market, here's what you're going to do next!" It doesn't work like that. This limitation is akin to predicting the behavior of a mischievous cat. We know broadly what a cat can and can't do. It can't fly, for instance, but it's nearly impossible to predict its antics on a moment-to-moment basis. It's the same idea with markets: we know broadly that they move in trends and follow long-term cycles shaped by macro- and microeconomic facts and expectations; yet the immediate twists and turns are a product of countless variables: headlines, individual investor sentiments, and even spontaneous reactions to technical chart points. Each market participant, equipped with their distinct experiences, strategies, and perceptions, contributes to the ever-shifting tapestry of market dynamics.

Hence, uncertainty is the reality of the market. This can't be said enough. Now, when one rigidly expects something from their analysis of a chaotic system like that, they are bound to get disappointed. Furthermore, they are bound to make strategic errors. The treacherous terrain is not the market itself but the realm of expectations, and the stronger the emotional ties to these expectations, the greater the risk of clouded judgment. The sheer weight of these emotions will distort the lens through which one views market movements.

Once again, stress, frustration, disappointment, and trading errors driven by those feelings and emotions stem from unmet expectations. It is imperative to understand this. And the mantra should be clear: observe, anticipate, but refrain from carving predictions in stone. Essentially, I'm emphasizing the indispensable need for a trader to possess enhanced mental and emotional adaptability. When you approach the markets, especially as a trend trader, entering a trade invariably involves a directional bias—either long or short. However, this prediction, integral as it is to the trading process, shouldn't cement your outlook. Upon executing a trade, it's crucial to shift gears mentally, adopting a more neutral stance. This means that while you've made an educated prediction, you acknowledge the core tenet: "I cannot be certain of the outcome." You should let go of any profit expectations you have for this trade and allow the market to take its course. It's akin to planting a seed and providing it with the necessary nutrients but understanding that nature ultimately decides its growth trajectory. This balanced perspective is not about undermining your initial judgment but rather about cultivating a sense of preparedness for all possible outcomes, with a particular emphasis on negative ones. Trading is a dynamic realm, and rigid expectations will often be a trader's downfall. By maintaining an agile mindset and following a rigid set of risk management rules, you're better equipped to navigate the unpredictable ebb and flow of the market.

Later, I'll introduce you to a little exercise that I found beneficial early in my trading journey when I was learning to grapple with the reality of uncertainty. Every time you place a trade, doing this little exercise will serve as a grounding ritual. Its primary purpose is to fortify the understanding within your psyche that, once your trade is placed, the eventual outcome is beyond your direct control. This will promote acceptance and ensure you remain anchored in reality rather than getting swept up in the tumultuous tides of hope or fear.

The Pathway to Profitability Amidst Uncertainty

Uncertainty—we have undeniably recognized it as a foundational characteristic of the market. Now, this raises the million-dollar question: Given uncertainty's ongoing presence, how does one consistently extract profits and craft an upward-trending equity curve? Is such a venture even within the realm of possibility? I'm here to affirmatively tell you that it is feasible. Not only am I doing this myself, but I've also witnessed numerous peers who've trodden a similar path with success. And to be clear, I'm not referring to momentary successes but sustainable profitability across a statistically substantial set of trades. Let's delve into the mechanics of achieving this. While the market's elusive nature doesn't offer any guarantees, there exists a set of foundational, time-tested principles that, when adhered to, tend to nudge you consistently toward profitable territory. This doesn't imply that every trade you initiate will result in profits; instead, it suggests that the trades you take will have a statistical edge, tilting the odds in your favor over time.

Firstly, consider the nature of trends. When a trend gains momentum, there's a potential—it's crucial to note that it's a potential and not a guarantee—for it to sustain its trajectory. This perspective parallels Newton's first law of motion, which posits that an object remains in its state of motion, preserving its speed, until some external force interferes. This fundamental physics concept echoes a time-tested trading wisdom: "The trend is your friend." Therefore, aligning your trades with overarching trends will tilt the odds in your favor because a dominant trend will often exert a guiding influence on lower time frames, and by aligning your trades with it, you position yourself favorably.

Next: proficient risk management must supersede prediction. Every successful trader wears the hat of a risk manager first. The mantra is simple—no catastrophic losses. The trading game is about survival; you must ensure your longevity in order to win. We'll tackle that point in greater length in the following segment.

Lastly, embrace the concept of profit asymmetry. While there's no harm in pocketing modest profits or even breaking even occasionally, periodically, you must provide the market space to transform some of your trades into significant wins. This approach not only elevates your average profits versus your average losses but also alleviates the pressure to perform. It cushions you against the inevitable losing streaks and keeps you on a positive trajectory (see Figure 2.11).

Now, underpinning these foundational principles is the idea of active engagement. True success in trading, like in life, is contingent upon the consistent yet calculated risks you're willing to undertake. If you refrain from engaging with the market, you're inadvertently sidelining yourself, preventing statistical advantages from manifesting in your favor. One foundational mathematical concept that underscores this is the Law of Large Numbers.

To distill the Law of Large Numbers, think of the simple act of tossing a fair coin with a twist in the payout structure: if it lands on heads, you gain $3, but if it's tails, you lose $1. While a single flip might yield an unpredictable outcome, flipping the coin multiple times will enable the realization of net positive gains. Even if the

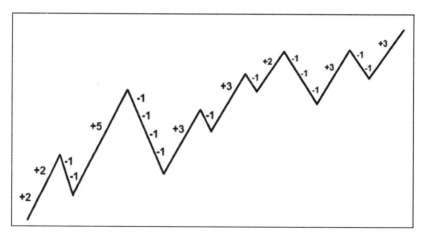

Figure 2.11 A trade management approach based on profit asymmetry will help you achieve a positive equity curve over time despite the uncertainty of which trades will win or lose.

coin lands on tails more often than on heads, the asymmetric risk-reward profile of the game will, over numerous flips, ensure that the numbers trend toward a profitable outcome. But you must stay long enough in the game; you must keep flipping that coin. Similarly, in trading, while individual trades are often fraught with uncertainty, consistently applying your strategy over many trades allows the statistical edge of that strategy to play out. As you stick with your strategy and continue engaging with the market, the numbers will generally trend toward a profitable outcome, as with the coin-flipping game.

As you see, this isn't rocket science. However, it must be understood that short-term outcomes are saturated with unpredictability and ambiguity. They are swayed by a multitude of factors, thereby making the outcome of a single trade, or even a small series of trades, somewhat erratic and potentially divergent from your strategy's profit potential. Consider a scenario where you enter a trade to go long; at that precise moment, the actions, strategies, and financial capabilities of hundreds of thousands of other market participants are unknowable to you. Your analyses might be spot-on from a broader perspective. Still, the market could dip in the short term, activating your stop loss and eliminating your position before eventually ascending in alignment with your initial analysis. Such scenarios are a frequent reality in trading, sowing seeds of frustration among traders and pushing them to think, "Perhaps ditching the stop loss is the way to go?" However, this could have dire repercussions, for the market does not always rebound, and a single instance of non-recovery can spell catastrophic outcomes, such as wiping out your account or triggering a margin call.

An alternative strategy to exit upon perceiving signs of a major breakdown is also fraught with issues as it leans heavily on the presumption that you can predict short-term market movements. It ignores the impossibly complex web of who is entering or exiting the market, their motivations, and their financial power. Suppose you are looking at volume and order flow and thinking, "Alright, there is a lot of buy interest at this level; I should go long." Another person might be looking at the same data and thinking: "I should probably countertrade this." You've identified a great trade entry point; another person could be looking at the same chart, same setup, same everything, and think: "I'll sell my position here to raise money for some much-needed vacation with my partner and kids." Do you see the conundrum of prediction? What you perceive as an opportunity to go long, informed by a MACD crossover, might be interpreted by another trader as a chance to go short or liquidate their current position. The core realization here is that every trader is maneuvering through the market, armed with their unique beliefs, goals, and expectations, and they express these through their actions in the market. However, beliefs, goals, and expectations often diverge significantly. The same data can signal vastly different actions to different traders. This variance in perspectives underscores the inherently chaotic nature of the market, a system where an unwavering level of uncertainty persists despite your analysis, strategy, and positions sometimes aligning and sometimes opposing the consensus.

Most traders can't accept the reality of uncertainty and relax amidst it. "Not knowing" profoundly destabilizes them on an emotional and psychological level. They are constantly craving certainty and in a perpetual pursuit of a tool, approach, or way of looking at the data that would dissipate the cloud of uncertainty. As depicted in the first chapter, I've been entwined in a similar struggle. As I embarked on this journey, I found myself encapsulated by the fantasy that I could come into the market daily and consistently secure profits. This fantasy held my perspective captive for years. I wasn't content with making more than I lose overall, in the aggregate; I wanted to take something home every day. And some days I did, but some days I didn't. When I didn't, it plummeted my mood, for my high expectations, when unmet, introduced a storm of disappointment. However, with continuous immersion and interaction with the market, a revelation slowly unfolded: the market, in its very nature, is beyond my control. Even with stringent adherence to my trading strategy, the market, much like the varying nature of weather—sometimes sun, sometimes rain—perpetually dances to its own rhythm. Surprisingly, once I reached this milestone in my evolution as a trader, genuinely internalizing that uncertainty, both intellectually and experientially, I started to come into my own as a trader, and my results got more and more consistent. This acceptance allowed me to relinquish my need to control the market and its short-term outcomes, instead anchoring my focus on the faithful application of my strategy and rules. I became less rigid with my expectations and more behaviorally consistent with my trading process.

Hence, change is possible. Not only is it possible, it is imperative. Mark my words, you will not succeed as trader without doing the hard but necessary work of accepting uncertainty. Your journey toward becoming a successful trader is inexorably linked to the acknowledgment and welcoming of uncertainty. By transforming your relationship with uncertainty, you lay down a solid foundation for making informed and strategic decisions in a realm where certainty is an illusion. Consequently, your trades, fueled not by anxiety or fear but by strategy and risk-conscious decisions, become reflections of a solidified trading identity. The journey ahead may be fraught with instances that test your resolve, yet with every trade, that persona will only get stronger and more refined. It's this identity that distinguishes seasoned traders from novices, a heightened level of confidence and composure that stems not from a delusion of control but from a profound respect and understanding of the uncertainty inherent in the market.

Moreover, as you keep maturing in your trading journey, you'll discover that your growth transcends beyond the confines of the market. You'll notice that it starts to seep into other realms of your life, nurturing a holistic development that defines you as a trader and shapes your worldview and interactions outside the trading world. The embrace of uncertainty becomes a philosophy, subtly guiding your decisions, approaches, and responses in various life scenarios. As you keep exploring the peaks and troughs, you gradually emerge as an illuminating example for other traders, demonstrating the balance that can be achieved amid the inherent chaos and unpredictability of both the market and life. Your journey, thus, becomes not only a personal victory but also a guiding light, ushering others toward the understanding that within the chaotic depths of uncertainty, strategic and mindful trading finds its true expression and test. This transformative journey is my wish for you, which is why I embarked on the mission of penning this book.

Making Peace with Uncertainty: The F.A.C.E Principle

I don't like the label "trader." It doesn't quite resonate with me; it's a loaded term and is embedded with varied connotations. In popular culture, traders are often portrayed in various ways; we're frequently viewed as prognosticators of the economy, leveraging our advanced chart-reading capabilities to forecast market trends; indeed, this entire industry rests on this predictive notion. Yet, there's another angle: as traders, we're also painted as gamblers, particularly on the retail end. It's a perspective not entirely without basis, as it arises from the hard truth that a substantial proportion of retail traders, unfortunately, do succumb to losses. Thus, to reiterate, the label "trader" doesn't quite capture my sentiments about the role. My preference leans toward the term "risk manager" because that is the crux of what we do. We engage with the market; we cap our risk in case things don't go as planned—and they often don't—we keep showing up with a proper attitude and perspective. In other words, we are not in the "prediction" business; we are in the "risk management" business.

Tangentially related, but converging toward a more significant notion I intend to convey: My partner and intimate circle of friends have affectionately dubbed me "The Uncertainty Guy" or "Mr. Uncertainty." This has become an internal jest among us because they perceive me as someone who incessantly talks about uncertainty, invariably weaving it into every conceivable conversation. While it's somewhat of an exaggeration—I don't think I always bring up uncertainty or intentionally steer conversations toward it—the observation itself is interesting. My engagement with, and frequent discourse on, uncertainty is deeply rooted in my own battles with embracing it, especially in the sphere of trading. That impassioned connection with the concept of uncertainty propelled me to explore it from myriad perspectives, whether scientific, probabilistic, spiritual, philosophical, or simply experiential. Consequently, I find myself perpetually enticed to converse about it because I see its reach in almost every facet of life. And herein lies the broader point: Uncertainty, in its rawest form, necessitates a surrender, a relinquishment of control, and a heartfelt acceptance of the boundless possibilities that arise when we allow life, or the market, in all its unpredictable splendor, to unfold organically. It's this very surrender, this acquiescence to the unknown, that cultivates a fertile ground where resilience takes root, where adaptability blossoms, where risk conscious deliberations mature, and where genuine growth is not merely possible but becomes an intrinsic part of our journey. Therefore, as "The Uncertainty Guy," my interactions, my philosophy, and indeed, my life, subtly aim to illuminate this perspective: Freedom lies in the embrace of the unknown.

As previously said, nearly every trading misstep originates from some form of an aversion to uncertainty. Take, for instance, the removal of your stop-loss with the anticipation that the market will pivot and gravitate back in your favored direction. This act embodies a clear-cut intolerance of uncertainty. It speaks to an expectation—a demand, even—that the market accommodates your needs and predictions. When hesitation seizes you, preventing you from executing your trades, it's a fear of the unknown casting its shadow over your actions. When you prematurely close a good trade, only to witness it ascend a few more percentage points shortly thereafter, it is your fear and inability to tolerate uncertainty that drives the action. The fear of missing out (FOMO) also intertwines with discomfort and nonacceptance of uncertainty. Here, you bypass your established trading process due to the apprehension of potentially overlooking a golden opportunity. Similarly, when overconfidence or complacency permeates your trading demeanor, it signals another variant of intolerance toward uncertainty. It's an illusion where you deceive yourself into believing that your knowledge of the market transcends its actual, inherently unpredictable nature.

To emphasize once again, most of the trading mistakes and resultant frustrations you'll encounter stem from a singular, erroneous expectation of the market—the expectation that it can provide something inherently unattainable, which is certainty or anything resembling it.

Consequently, the pivotal question emerges: How does one embrace uncertainty? How does one make peace with it? Reflecting on this, I'm reminded of an episode from my life. Once, amid a meditation retreat, I found myself feeling particularly restless. Seeking solace, I stepped away from the confines of the meditation hall and ventured out into nature for a little walk. As I observed the world around me, the omnipresence of uncertainty, even in nature, dawned on me. The unpredictable gusts of wind, the sudden rain showers, the erratic flight pattern of birds, the different sounds popping up here and there; nature was full of uncertainties, yet there was a grace in how it all unfolded. This realization set me on a journey to truly understand how to navigate and thrive amidst life's uncertainties with greater grace. I started reflecting on my experiences in the market and the emotions and rationale behind some of the decisions that I made that got me to where I was. After months of introspection, my insights eventually crystallized into a framework. It was not just a theoretical construct; I employed it upon my return to the trading world after my meditation sojourn, and the outcomes were nothing short of remarkable.

Inspired by these transformative insights, and driven by a desire to empower others in their journey, I started sharing this framework on social media, breaking it down for easy comprehension. While the essence of what I shared is not novel—many traders before me have emphasized the significance of embracing uncertainty—their explanations often lacked the simplicity and directness necessary for a more universal grasp. Therefore, the clarity and distinctiveness of my approach were met with resounding appreciation from fellow traders and enthusiasts.

To further streamline this knowledge, I encapsulated it into a mnemonic that, if applied with sincerity and discipline, will serve as a beacon for traders navigating the stormy seas of markets.

I named it F.A.C.E., an apt reminder that the key to success is facing uncertainty head-on.

F.A.C.E. stands for:

- F: Fully Embracing Reality
- A: Appreciating the Statistical Nature of Trading
- C: Centering on Survival
- E: Easing Off the Prediction Paradigm

Before we embark on a detailed exploration of each element of F.A.C.E., it's vital to understand that it's more than just an acronym. F.A.C.E. is a philosophy, a mindset, a compass. At its heart, it is about equipping oneself with the right mental framework for trading and life. F.A.C.E. is about embracing uncertainty with strategy and grace. F.A.C.E. arms you with the right perspectives to foster not just market success but also personal growth and mental resilience. Hence, as we navigate F.A.C.E.'s intricacies, I invite you to internalize its game-changing principles.

F: Fully Embracing Reality

It's crucial to recognize and openly admit the omnipresence of uncertainty in trading. The markets, with their inherent variability and unforeseen fluctuations, will always harbor unknowns that you cannot control. When you place a trade, someone halfway around the globe might interpret the same data in an entirely different way. And if that person places an order opposite to yours, and with sufficient financial power, they will move the market and invalidate your trade. While it's true that market trends and cycles are broadly predictable, since the global macroeconomic forces that shape markets are themselves broadly predictable, on a trade-by-trade basis, anything can happen. Anything! We know that markets respond to technical levels on charts, but we are in the dark about which ones will hold and the magnitude of the reaction. The market might effortlessly cut through a primary support only to rebound from a less significant one or breach a major resistance and be halted by the upper limit of a minor trendline. The intricate dynamics of the market, driven by myriad factors, continuously shape and reshape these patterns, often in ways that defy logical prediction or pattern recognition (see Figure 2.12).

Acknowledging the persistent reality of uncertainty is the first stride toward establishing a balanced and harmonious relationship with it. However, the entirety of the trading industry appears obsessed with forecasting the market's next move. Financial experts, trading gurus, and media pundits alike all bask in this false idea of certainty. Declarations like, "Apple will hit this target by this time" or "Bitcoin will reach this value by then" are rampant. Such predictions are foolish. The idea of predicting an exact figure within a specific time frame is beyond the realm of human capability. Essentially, it would require a being with unlimited presence and power; in other words, a God. And let's face it, we are all just human. We are susceptible to mistakes, biases, and imperfections. Hence, it's important to adopt a humble stance in our predictions. The significance of humility in trading cannot be overstated because the market will repeatedly prove you wrong, presenting you with losses when you least expect them. Absent a quality of humility? Know

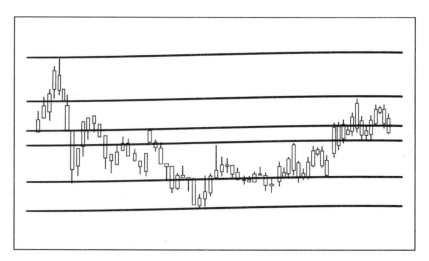

Figure 2.12 This figure showcases the dynamic nature of the market, where support and resistance levels are continually being reshaped and redefined.

this: Consistency will remain elusive, and you won't survive long enough to experience lasting success.

Humility doesn't translate to a lack of confidence; rather, it refers to the earnest acknowledgment that the market can and will surprise us despite our best strategies and analysis. To have humility in trading is to have the awareness that our understanding of the market is perpetually partial and that our trades are always subject to forces beyond our comprehension and control. There's an intrinsic beauty and strength in humility. In being humble, you align yourself with the erratic ebb and flow of the market, understanding that every trade is a risk and that each outcome, win or lose, is a chance to learn and grow. This perspective not only molds you into a more resilient trader but also a perpetual learner and student of uncertainty. Furthermore, humility enables you to trade without the weighty burden of ego, which can often cloud judgment and lead to riskier decisions in a bid to prove yourself right.

In your journey ahead, continuously recognize the unwavering presence of uncertainty within the markets. Rather than tensing against it, learn to relax into it. Foster a continuous sense of humility. Become a student of the markets' rhythms rather than an adversary. This signifies a transition from a conflict model—me against the market—to a harmony model, where you and the market exist in an almost symbiotic relationship. It's a simple shift in perspective; however, understand that it is not without its challenges. It's essential to remember that every fiber of your being instinctively seeks predictability; your innate nature is to anticipate the future. This makes the task of truly accepting and internalizing uncertainty a continual endeavor. Hence, every market engagement should be an opportunity to proactively adjust your mindset, steering it toward welcoming uncertainty.

Several years back, as you might recall from the first chapter, I underwent an eye-opening event that laid bare the intricate workings of my mind. Fresh from a half-year-long sabbatical dedicated solely to deep meditation on retreats, I was slowly reintegrating into society. Jobless and confronted with the pressing need to earn, I found myself gravitating back to trading. This was despite the stinging memories of past failures I had faced in this very arena. With a fresh new outlook on life and an introspective tool like meditation to help me cope with the ups and downs of the market, I was ready and determined to make trading work this time. However, looking at my trading account and records, I was suddenly overwhelmed by a crushing feeling of anxiety running throughout my entire body. My past failures were still haunting me—over five years, I had burned down a $100,000 trading account and was left to work with about $14,000. The challenge was immense, but I was steadfast in my resolve. I knew I couldn't let my trauma—fears and anxieties—take the front seat, or else I would doom myself once again. With that in mind, I embarked on a personal experiment: every day for a few weeks, I made fearlessness amidst uncertainty the object of my morning introspective routine. Here's how it went: every sunrise, after shaking off sleep, I would meditate to set my mind in the right direction for the trading day. After the session, feeling calmer and more grounded, I would journal my reflections on the ever-present uncertainty that permeates the market, and more broadly, life. The writing, free-flowing and unburdened by overthinking, was transformative as it enabled the forging of connections between diverse insights; it also aided structured thinking, which helped me better integrate the lessons on uncertainty that the market handed me. Over time, I became less perturbed by uncertainty because that ongoing work of self-awareness and reflection and consistent engagement with the market helped me build a repertoire of positive experiences with uncertainty, embedding it deeply into my overarching life philosophy.

Facing uncertainty is challenging, and if you find yourself in this struggle, I highly advise doing this little introspective routine for a few weeks at the very least. Drawing from my years of guiding traders, I can assure you that this practice will significantly alter your perspective on uncertainty. We'll explore the meditation component in Chapter 3. As for the journaling one, here's a suggested framework to ensure you get the most out of it:

1. Writing Prompts

Every day, write down the following prompts in your journal:

- "Today, I cannot predict . . ."
- "If I were more accepting of uncertainty, how would I approach my trading?"
- "I am prepared for the unexpected in the market today by . . ."

For each prompt, jot down your thoughts. This might look something like:

- "Today, I cannot predict how the market will react to the latest news update."
- "If I were more accepting of uncertainty, I wouldn't berate myself for not catching exact tops or bottoms."
- "I am fully prepared for the unexpected in the market today by sticking with my stop losses."

2. Reflection and Acceptance

After completing your entries, take a moment to read them aloud to yourself. However, make sure that you're not merely paying lip service or mindlessly repeating them. I've seen a lot of traders do this—they read interesting books on trading psychology and then go around parroting the concepts without genuinely believing them. Unfortunately, mindless parroting won't suffice! For your actions to truly align with the principles I'm discussing here, you must hold a profound, internal belief in them. Hence, as you take a moment to recite what you wrote, breathe deeply and feel the weight of the uncertainty. Accept it mindfully. Befriend it. Understand that it's an inherent part of the trading world.

3. Post-Trading Reflection

At the end of your trading day, revisit your journal. Reflect on how your day went in relation to your morning entries. Did you remain mindful of the uncertainty? Were you able to maintain a calm and adaptable mindset in the face of the unexpected? Were you able to stick to your trading process?

Every trading psychology technique and strategy I offer my clients stems from the experience I've gathered over the years as a trader and as a coach and mentor. I've noticed a profound transformation in clients who genuinely engage with the idea of navigating uncertainty. When they ask themselves questions like "If I were more accepting of uncertainty, how would I approach this situation?" and then weave that perspective into their trading and daily lives, the results are truly remarkable. Challenges stemming from an inability to accept uncertainty begin to fade. Gradually, they come to terms with this inherent aspect of the market. By jotting down their reflections, they discern patterns in their responses and mindsets, making it easier to address any persistent biases or fears. If you're aiming to bolster your ability to handle uncertainty, this practice is invaluable. Foster an identity as a trader who thrives amidst uncertainty and make it a cornerstone of your worldview. To quote the Mandalorian, "This is the way."

A: Appreciating the Statistical Nature of Trading

As said earlier, trading is a statistical probability game. That's all it is. There are stakes, there are potential rewards, and then there's uncertainty. But despite that uncertainty, if you diligently adhere to a robust trading strategy or system, you stand a good chance of prevailing over time. Put another way, you can win as a trader if you focus on playing the numbers game. And playing the numbers game demands that you avoid getting emotionally involved in the process. It necessitates a certain level of emotional detachment. Now, I get it. That is usually not much of an epiphany to people. It's not enough to try to convince yourself that uncertainty is going to be fine if you follow your trading strategy or system. It's not even enough for me to sit here in my office, pour my heart into this book, trying to make it simple yet compelling enough for those concepts to land. It's not enough. The crux lies in confronting uncertainty head-on and observing the outcome. We develop our individual resilience to uncertainty not by trying to sidestep it but by diving deep into it, examining our responses, and checking if our worries and apprehensions materialize. It's a process of getting to know that uncertainty and befriending it. Once again, it's a deliberate act of leaning into the unknown instead of reflexively shying away from it.

Analogies can be invaluable in this journey. They offer clarity by drawing parallels to familiar situations, helping us grasp and integrate complex or elusive ideas. With the right analogy, what might seem like an intimidating or vague concept can suddenly click into place, offering a fresh perspective and deeper understanding. On that note, here are two analogy-driven exercises that I highly recommend you undertake. The real value in doing them is crystallizing these concepts in your mind so they start to structure how you approach the market.

Exercise 1: Coin Flip

Objective: Understand the concept of expected value and how it plays out over repeated trials.

Materials: Coins, paper, pen.

Setup:

I strongly recommend you carry out this exercise with a partner or friend using real money. One will be the "Market," and the other will be the "Trader."

For every coin flip that results in heads, award the trader $2. Conversely, for every coin flip that ends up as tails, the trader must give the market $1. Keeping the stakes real is essential: if the trader incurs a loss (owing $1 to the market for tails), it must be considered a genuine loss; therefore, there should be no reimbursement afterward. Stick to the rules and maintain the integrity of the exercise.

Procedure:

The market always flips the coin.

The results are noted after each flip.

After 50 rounds, the trader calculates their net balance.

Evaluation:

What is your ending balance? How did it feel with each win or loss? Were there streaks of consecutive wins or losses? How did they impact your emotions or anticipation for the next flip? How would you feel if the stakes were higher? What are the parallels between this game and trading? Write down your thoughts.

Exercise 2: Card Betting

Objective: Understand risk management and how big losses can derail your performance

    Materials: Standard decks of playing cards, paper, pen.

Setup:

As with the first exercise, I suggest you carry out the exercise with a partner or friend using actual money. One person assumes the role of the "Market," while the other becomes the "Trader."

    If the trader draws a red card (heart or diamond), it's considered a "bullish" market, and if they draw a black card (club or spade), it's a "bearish" market.

    If the trader bets on bullish and draws a red card, they gain \$3; if they bet on a bearish and draw a black card, they gain \$3. If they're wrong, they lose \$1.

    When the trader draws a Joker, it's a \$15 loss; when they draw a second Joker, it's a \$30 loss.

    Keep the stakes real. A loss is a loss—give it to the market and don't take it back. Stick to the rules to maintain the exercise's integrity and help crystallize those concepts in your mind.

Procedure:

The trader bets on bullish or bearish until there are no cards left to draw.

    Payouts are made according to the rules.

    The results are noted after each flip.

    When no cards are left, calculate net balances.

Evaluation:

What is your ending balance? How did it feel with each win or loss? Did you experience any streaks of consecutive wins or losses? How did the substantial losses caused by drawing Joker cards affect your overall balance? How did these losses influence your emotions? Can you identify any similarities between this game and trading? Write down your thoughts.

* * *

The primary purpose of these exercises is multifaceted: To begin with, they leverage hands-on learning—through actions like flipping coins or drawing cards and the tangible exchange of money—and social dynamics—one person on each side of the bets—to solidify in a more visceral way core concepts that are at play in trading.

Next, the exercises underscore that even if predicting individual outcomes remains elusive, one can develop a broader understanding of probabilistic patterns anchored by the pivotal idea of "expected value." This concept offers a glimpse into your potential long-term returns or losses: it tells you the average amount you would expect to win (or lose) per play if you kept playing the game many times. We've discussed this previously, so there's no need to revisit it. For traders, grasping the concept of expected value and emphasizing it allows for an evaluation of the potential success of their strategies, or even specific trades, over multiple transactions rather than being overly concerned with the result of a single trade.

Thirdly, the exercises underline the importance of risk management. It's one thing to theoretically grasp the merits of risk management, but seeing and feeling that concept play out solidifies it in a visceral way. Then, tied closely to the concept of risk is the potential for reward since risk and opportunity are two sides of the same coin. Closely linked to risk is reward potential. In trading, occasional small gains or break-even situations are acceptable. However, it's vital to ensure that successful trades occasionally deliver more substantial gains, thereby enhancing the average profit compared to the average loss. This approach lessens the reliance on a high win rate to succeed, thus easing the performance expectations placed on the trader.

Fourthly, throughout these exercises, you're nudged into a whirlwind of emotions, albeit subdued compared to actual trading scenarios. From exhilaration during a winning streak to the distress following a series of losses, or even fleeting doubts, acknowledging and mastering these emotions is crucial for trading success. These exercises pave the path toward an amplified awareness of the necessity for emotional fortitude amidst the unpredictable swings of trade outcomes.

Fifth, as you do these exercises, there's an opportunity to discern some of your behavioral patterns. Perhaps a series of losses might prompt an overwhelming desire to predict a win next, or consistent wins could lead to the presumption of an imminent loss. These insights are crucial, highlighting the psychological pitfalls traders frequently encounter. By recognizing these tendencies in a controlled environment, strategies can be devised to sidestep them in real trading situations. We'll delve deeper into these strategies in the subsequent chapters.

Lastly, the exercises serve as a reminder that we don't control the outcomes. A lot of people underestimate the fact that outcomes tend to cluster, even when dealing with strategies that boast a high win rate. They also underestimate the frequency of those clusters. They expect the number of losses to follow a predictable, linear pattern based on historical data sets. However, in the dynamic world of trading, past performance doesn't always predict future results, and expecting a straightforward trajectory can lead to unrealistic expectations and subsequent disappointments. Hence, while we can't control outcomes, we can firmly control our expectations and reactions to them. This shift from a focus on results to a focus on the process is a hallmark of seasoned traders. They understand that while individual trades can be unpredictable, having a sound strategy and managing their reactions can lead to consistent success over time. By embedding this process-oriented mindset, you're setting the foundation for a more disciplined and rational approach to trading.

Now, of course, trading is certainly more multidimensional than a coin flip or card game, but the core principles are the same. There are risks and rewards, and given the omnipresence of uncertainty, how one frames the risks versus the rewards is what predominantly determines the expected value of the game. Keep this at the forefront of your mind as you journey deeper into the intricacies of this endeavor. One last important note: outcomes often group together—profits or losses tend to cluster. Grasping this concept is vital to maintaining your composure, especially when market dynamics aren't tilting in your favor. You will often diligently stick to your trading strategy and still face a series of losses. This simply means that the current market phase isn't aligning with your approach. Occasionally, this misalignment may persist for just a single trading session, but in other instances, it might extend for days or even weeks. Even though profits might seem sporadic, it's imperative to remain disciplined and persistent, trusting that your strategy will eventually have its day.

C: Centering on Survival

As noted in the opening chapter, I've taken on the responsibility of managing a small fund in recent years. I say "small" because, in the grand scheme, the amount we're working with—a few million—is a mere speck in the vast ocean of institutional finance. That being said, for the longest time, the very idea of trading on behalf of others was a line I was reluctant to cross. The gravity of that responsibility, combined with the weight of potential losses and the inevitable difficult conversations that might follow, always deterred me. By nature, I lean toward introversion; hence, I've always found it difficult to engage in intense or challenging discussions. My stutter, a challenge I've grappled with my entire life, makes the prospect of those conversations even more daunting. However, a couple of years ago, I took the plunge; curiously, it was right before the world turned upside down with COVID. The turning point wasn't a newfound confidence in my skills but an epiphany about communication. I grasped that I could manage other people's investments if I were transparent and candid from the outset, ensuring that all involved fully understood the venture's potential risks and rewards.

Nowadays, before anyone joins the ranks of my fund's investors, we have a real sit-down. It's not just about the paperwork or the formalities; it's a heart-to-heart about what they're looking for, their comfort with risk, and what's actually doable in the trading world. I lay it out straight: I don't have a crystal ball. I'm not the guy who will call the exact tops and bottoms or even the daily ups and downs of the market. I'm no oracle or fortune teller. Instead of predicting exact market movements, I focus on identifying instances where trends could emerge or resume. When I've identified such an instance, I jump in. But perhaps more importantly, I have measures in place to manage the risk in case things don't pan out as antici-pated, which is often the case. In other words, I'm an expert risk manager, not an expert predictor. It's a non-negotiable criterion for me that potential investors in our fund understand this principle. If they're under the illusion that I'm some sort of a Nostradamus, then it's a hard no from me. Their money stays with them, and they don't get to invest in the fund. Even if they have a few million in a suit-case. This stringent screening process has been a lifesaver, sparing me from working with people who don't have the right perspective or expectations. The people I do decide to collaborate with are well aware that my realm isn't predicting the unpredictable; it's effec-tively managing risks. Their expectations are then finely tuned to the market's true nature, entirely at ease with its inherent uncer-tainties and potential losses. Essentially, these investors entrust me with their funds to skillfully navigate the market's waters, minimiz-ing potential pitfalls while maximizing growth opportunities. It's about maneuvering uncertainty methodically, with precision, pro-fessionalism, and intellect, always keeping their best interests at the forefront.

This can't be emphasized enough: Markets move in trends, and one of our goals as traders is to pinpoint moments when a trend might emerge or continue. This isn't a given. The word "might" is pivotal here, suggesting a mere possibility. Not everything goes according to plan—welcome to the reality of trading! Being wrong is something we all have to face more often than we would like. That is where the essence of smart risk management comes into play. Smart risk management means taking risks that, even if they result in consecutive losses, won't jeopardize our staying power. This is key—continued engagement with the market. The main goal in trading isn't to make a quick win but to stay in for the long haul. Indeed, the mantra "success comes from showing up" rings particularly true here. The ability to (1) remain in the game, (2) seize market opportunities while keeping losses manageable, and (3) do it with a proper attitude is what truly sets successful traders apart. By managing risk and staying in the game, one increases their chances of being at the right place and time for lucrative market opportunities. However, if one trades with positions that are too large, they will end up getting pushed out of the game sooner than they'd like.

Another aspect of continued engagement with the market is the exposure to rare but exceptional opportunities, and importantly, without ever having to bet the farm. By continually showing up, armed with a sound process or strategy, the market will inevitably offer instances where the asymmetry of the bet is largely skewed toward profit—sometimes as high as 1,000 to 1. The risk on such bets is often so far outweighed that you could almost label them "risk-free trades." Of course, there is no such thing as a risk-free trade; there are no free lunches in the market, but that is as close to it as you will get. Imagine this: putting a mere couple thousand on the line with the potential to yield hundreds of thousands, even millions. Where else can you do that—turn tiny grubstakes into substantial amounts? That is the beauty of the market; that is what makes trading so unique. Trade long enough and you will capture one, or maybe even a handful of these opportunities. It's important to highlight that these opportunities don't come around often. They're elusive and hard to anticipate. In my years of being active in the market, I've captured maybe five of these opportunities, but their impact on my performance has been nothing short of transformational. They have punctuated my otherwise boring but gradual upward equity trajectory with notable surges. Hence, this is why survival and ongoing engagement with the market is paramount.

It is this very engagement that brings to the forefront those dia-monds in the rough, which, when seized, can be game-changers in a trader's journey.

A brief word on what constitutes good risk management prac-tices. There's a lot of chatter out there about the "right" amount to risk on a trade. Some suggest not going beyond 1% of your capital, others recommend 0.5%, and there are those who even go up to 5% or more. My take? It's not a one-size-fits-all scenario. The optimal risk percentage largely hinges on one's specific strategy, one's goals, and quite honestly, one's comfort with risk. It's imperative to factor in both personal circumstances and your own understanding of what you seek from the market. Risk management isn't purely black and white. On the one hand, it has a subjective side, rooted in one's individual preferences, objectives, and risk comfort level. On the other hand, there's an undeniable objective component centered around market probabilities. For instance, both winning and losing trades tend to cluster. Risk too much, and a few consecutive losses could severely deplete your capital, leaving you unable to continue trading. This objective reality of trading dynamics is something you can't ignore in your risk management strategy.

From my stance, here's my approach to risk management: At any given moment, I can have up to 50 trades active since, in my trading, I put a lot of emphasis on playing the numbers game. Typically, I allocate between 0.5% to 1% of my total account as posi-tion size for each trade. This allocation strategy allows me to set my stop losses based on crucial market parameters, like major support or resistance levels, rather than arbitrary thresholds like percent-ages or personal monetary concerns. That approach prevents me from getting stopped out of trades unnecessarily. But even when I do get stopped out, my losses are negligible due to the minimal percentage I have staked—remember, I'm only using 0.5% to 1% of my total account as position size for each trade. Hence, say I'm in a long position, and the stock goes to zero. Well, that would barely scratch the surface of my account. There is an undeniable advan-tage in trading large accounts, as you can see; however, I'm well aware that not everyone has deep pockets to begin with; my own journey began modestly. The point is, rather than getting hung up on generic risk guidelines that permeate the Internet, it's essential to tailor your risk management approach to your personal goals, risk appetite, financial situation, and trading strategy.

I genuinely hope to cement this concept deeply in your mind. It is crucial to be methodical in managing your risks. Rarely will you find traders claiming they practiced sound risk management, took minor losses, and still depleted their accounts entirely. More often, you'll hear the opposite—they took significant risks and blew up. They treat trading as a thrill, seeking excitement. Such an attitude is a recipe for losses. Therefore, stand out from the majority. Position your trades so you won't lose your shirt if something doesn't go as planned. When the market is about to hit your risk control threshold, detach from wishful thinking. Take the loss; live to fight other battles. Keep engaging the market; keep flipping that metaphorical coin with a proper attitude and long-term perspective. Envision trading as a gradual ascent to wealth, not an instant jackpot. While the ascent to success will likely be gradual, it will make it almost a given.

E: Easing Off the Prediction Paradigm

If you don't accept uncertainty and are bent on predicting exact tops and bottoms or even trade outcomes, there's a good chance you're on the losing side more often than not. Most beginning traders are unknowingly taught methods that inherently champion such a predictive approach. This prevalent paradigm, which dominates much of the trading industry, is not without its repercussions. Such an approach inevitably cultivates an emotional bond with trade outcomes, leading to behavioral inconsistency and a cascade of trading missteps. This is predominantly because their mindset clashes with the very essence of the market, which is wrapped in layers of uncertainty.

Trend traders typically put their trades on with a directional inclination. This is normal; prediction is baked into the endeavor of trading. The issue is that most traders don't balance their predictions with a thorough understanding, appreciation, and embrace of uncertainty. While it's entirely reasonable to anticipate market movement, the moment your trade is active, it's crucial to relinquish any attempts to forecast its result. Although this may seem conflicting, even paradoxical, it becomes clear when you delve deeper. As previously mentioned, once your position is in the market, it becomes susceptible to a multitude of factors that are beyond your control. The market is a dynamic entity, constantly influenced by micro and macro events and economic circumstances, along with the collective psychology of millions of participants. Even though your directional bias might be correct, your trade can be easily disrupted by these unpredictable variables. Consider the vast number of participants operating simultaneously, each with their own strategies, perspectives, insights, and motivations. Just one major player, be it an institutional investor or a whale, making a move contrary to your trade can trigger a cascade of reactions in the market. This ripple effect can amplify and eventually invalidate your trade without even disrupting your directional prediction for the market (see Figure 2.13).

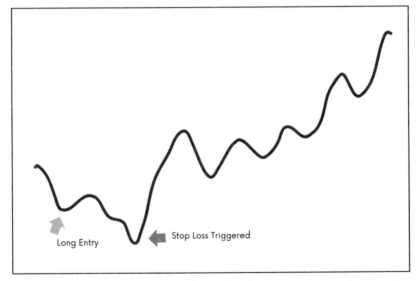

Figure 2.13   Your trade can still result in a loss despite an accurate directional bias. Welcome to uncertainty!

Given this uncertainty, it's essential to detach emotionally from your trade once it is placed. Let me repeat this for emphasis: it is essential to detach emotionally from your trade once it is placed. Of course, this is exceedingly challenging for many traders because, in their minds, they're reasoning, "Based on my analysis, the price should rise . . .Thus, I ought to gain if I take a long position." On paper, it sounds straightforward; however, the catch is that once you opt for a long position, for example, it's impossible to predict the actions of the myriad of other traders at that precise moment. You can't discern who is buying or selling in the near term, nor their motivations or financial power. While your broad analysis might be spot on, the market might initially move in the opposite direction, triggering your stop loss, wiping out your position, only to rally later in the direction you anticipated. This scenario is all too familiar, leading to significant frustration for traders.

Some might then conclude, "I'll just skip using a stop loss." That perspective poses its own set of challenges. All it requires is one situation—just one—where the market doesn't bounce back. The fallout can be severe, potentially decimating your account or triggering a margin call (see Figure 2.14).

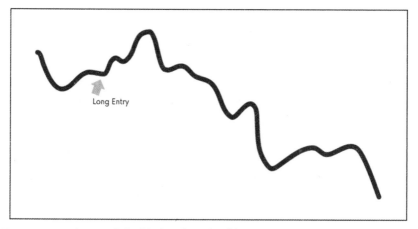

Figure 2.14 This graph highlights the risk of foregoing a stop loss, hoping that the market recovers.

Then, they might argue, "I'll just exit once I perceive major indicators of a collapse or when the chart seems off." But therein lies yet another issue. This approach is predicated on the assumption that you can accurately predict short-term market movements. In reality, it's impossible to know with certainty at any given time. You can't reliably pinpoint who's joining or departing the market, their reasons, or their financial clout. Hence, a situation that appears to be a bearish downturn to you might be interpreted entirely differently by another trader. Remember, we are all trading our expectations, and we convey these expectations with where and how we decide to deploy our capital. Expectations frequently differ among traders, and this divergence is what makes the market the chaotic system that it is.

Given this backdrop, approaching market analysis requires a nuanced perspective, as those who consistently see profits can attest. Firstly, in regard to technical analysis, which encompasses elements like price pattern analysis, technical indicators, and the identification of support and resistance levels, alongside trend and volume analysis, it's important to understand what it can and can't do. These methodologies and instruments grant insights into trends, areas for buying and selling, and prospective price shifts. While markets have a fractal nature and respond to these technical markers, it's vital to understand that one cannot precisely pinpoint which levels the price will gravitate toward or the magnitude of its response. Hence, rather than viewing technical analysis as a means of foretelling the market's every move, savvy traders perceive it as a tool to streamline risk management. In essence, technical analysis serves as a mechanism to determine stop-loss points, identify feasible entry and exit junctures, and calibrate position sizes to shield from unforeseen market volatilities. Hence, to reiterate, technical analysis is about risk mitigation. Adopting this perspective is crucial—it's less about forecasting and more about strategizing around uncertainties.

Following technical analysis, order flows are also a tool many traders hold in high regard. They grant a window into the market's buying and selling activities, shedding light on prevailing sentiments and actions of major players and institutions. Some might categorize this within the realm of technical analysis, but regardless of how it's labeled, its true value lies in its application. However, here's a caveat: some market participants use a practice called "spoofing," especially those with deep pockets. Spoofing is a tactic where conspicuous orders are placed, not with the intention of executing them, but to manipulate. Once these deceptive orders are active or soon after being withdrawn, they're counteracted with an order of the opposite kind. Several forms of spoofing exist, but the essence of it, regardless of its variations, is to create "pretend orders" to project a particular narrative for other participants about market direction. Sophisticated players use this strategy as a way to manipulate perceptions to secure favorable entry points. For instance, if they want to countertrade the consensus, they manipulate perception with these proof orders to get more favorable entry prices. In other scenarios, when they're looking to exit a long position, they may skew the order books to project that buyers have the upper hand. This deception lures in naive participants, briefly inflating prices and providing a more liquid environment for the manipulator to sell. The point is, order books aren't foolproof. Similar to technical analysis, they are not a predictive oracle. Should one decide to use them, they must approach them with awareness and risk control.

Lastly, there is fundamental analysis. This method seeks to discern the intrinsic value of an asset, which, it's important to note, is more of an approximation rather than a precise figure. To achieve this, one has to sift through various data points, including both macro- and microeconomic indicators. However, a dose of realism is necessary—fundamental analysis, too, isn't infallible. The perceived intrinsic value of an asset may not always align with market valuations. Hence, you might find stellar companies being valued at a premium that seems unjustified. The value of fundamental analysis lies in its ability to inform long-term investments, giving traders confidence in their holdings' inherent worth. However, it's essential to marry this analysis with a deep respect for the unpredictable nature of the markets.

Consider this: We humans have an innate tendency to crave control. It is arguably a deep-seated urge that pushes us to dominate our surroundings and shape our future. This impulse leads many traders to believe they can decipher and outsmart the market by predicting its every move. However, realizing that the market remains indifferent to our analysis, strategies, or aspirations is pivotal. Instead of striving to "conquer" or "outsmart" the market, approach it with a more holistic perspective. Engage with the above trading tools and methods, but always keep in mind the broader context of the market and all the other variables that remain shrouded in mystery. Maintain humility in the face of the ever-present uncertainty. Many traders, unfortunately, view the market as an adversary, setting up a "me versus it" scenario. This mindset forces a predictive outlook and personalizes trades, adding an emotional weight that clouds judgment, more often than not. Elevated expectations, when unmet, lead to inevitable frustrations and trading missteps. It's no wonder, then, that the vast majority of retail traders are on the losing side. A staggering 90% of them end up losing according to some statistics (Rolf 2019). The culprit is this prediction paradigm, coupled with an inability to manage their emotions. To succeed, you need a fresh approach, one that's distinct from the conventional mindset, and the outcomes will naturally be different.

Earlier, I said that I would share a little exercise that I've found beneficial in my own trading, when I was learning to grapple with the reality of uncertainty. Here it is: when I placed a trade, I would flip a coin. Simple as it sounds, the act served a deeper purpose. It reshaped my mindset, reminding me of the inherent uncertainty in every decision. Furthermore, it's worth noting that, unlike our interactions with the market, when flipping a coin, we don't typically do it with ego. We don't plead for it to land on heads or tails because we understand its outcome is beyond our influence; it's pure chance. But in trading, our passionate reading of charts biases us into believing that the market should mirror our predictions. When it doesn't, we're often left feeling wronged, frustrated, even betrayed. This emotional response highlights a misalignment in our expectations. They don't match the market's inherent nature. But seeing each trade akin to a coin toss helps recalibrate these expectations. It's a subtle yet powerful gesture of acknowledging the uncertain essence of the market. It's your way of affirming, "I recognize you, uncertainty, and I won't be blindsided."

Admittedly, it's challenging to place a trade, knowing it might not pan out. But that is the nature of the game we're playing. Sometimes your mind will be screaming, "This trade will be a sure loser," and next thing you know, it's a winner. And the opposite is also true: sometimes your mind will be screaming, "This trade will be a profitable trade," and next thing you know, it's a loser. Hence, viewing each trade through the coin-flip lens is a tangible acknowledgment of the market's inherent uncertainty. It's accepting that the future remains shrouded in mystery. Hence, every time you place a trade, do this little exercise. It will serve as a grounding ritual. It will fortify the understanding within your psyche that, once your trade is placed, the eventual outcome is beyond your direct control. This will promote acceptance and ensure that you remain anchored in reality and risk management rather than swayed by whimsical dreams or fears.

As our exploration has highlighted, the F.A.C.E. principle underscores the inevitability and omnipresence of uncertainty in our lives. Be it in trading decisions or life choices, this framework offers a compass to navigate the chaos with structure and consistency. By Fully embracing reality, Appreciating the statistical nature of trading, Centering on survival, and Easing off the prediction paradigm, we are equipped mentally and strategically to not just survive but also thrive amidst the ups and downs of things. Remember: making peace with uncertainty doesn't mean eliminating it. One doesn't need to predict the market's every move to achieve consistent trading success. Let me say it again for emphasis: success in trading doesn't hinge on predicting every twist and turn in the market! Grasping this concept is a transformative revelation because it showcases the importance of a structured approach and a disciplined mindset. Hence, the F.A.C.E. mnemonic is not just a set of abstract ideas; it is a lived experience, a dynamic practice that can transform the very essence of one's approach to the market. Through its diligent application, our rapport with uncertainty shifts from a nerve-wracking challenge to a catalyst for potential and growth. However, it's essential to note that the F.A.C.E. framework's efficacy is contingent on having a sound trading system or strategy in place. This might seem like an obvious point, but it warrants emphasis. This book is tailored with the belief that you possess such a strategy. Given this foundation, embodying the F.A.C.E. principle will empower you to face tomorrow's uncertainties with confidence and grace.

Random or Not: That Is the Question

From our journey so far, one might conclude that I'm advocating for a view that everything is entirely up to chance. That couldn't be further from the truth. Contrarily, I don't view the market, or life for that matter, as being completely random. In my opinion, the notion of things appearing "random" stems more from the gaps in our understanding than from the actual nature of events themselves. I'm a determinist at heart. Determinism is the philosophical stance that every occurrence, including human choices and behaviors, is inevitably shaped by preceding events or determinants. This posits that we exist within an intricate, vast web of cause and effect, so expansive and convoluted that our finite minds struggle to grasp its entirety.

If we were to journey through the annals of time, we'd recognize a sequence of events meticulously leading to our present. This is but a brief snapshot of the events that occurred: Everything begins with nothingness: From this impossible-to-conceptualize, "nothingness" erupts a burst of immense energy, giving birth to an ever-expanding universe. Originating from a dimensionless, eternal singularity, this universe grows and morphs, governed by a handful of unwavering deterministic laws. Particles dance and merge, forming atoms. These atoms come together to birth molecules, and soon, these molecules begin crafting the perceivable reality we know.

Chaos subtly transitions into order, laying the foundation for celestial bodies: stars are kindled, and much later, planets coalesce. Now, something even more miraculous happens. On a tiny, seemingly inconsequential orb, the once-inanimate matter begins a transformative journey toward life. What once was simple now grows in complexity, exhibiting consciousness—a capability to sense, to feel, to experience existence. And as the journey continues, humans emerge. The intricate web of cause and effect, possibly absent of overt intent, results in our being. We are unique arrangements of atoms and molecules, cosmic melodies if you will, finding our place in this boundless and perhaps purposeless universe. At our core, we are but matter with an illusory sense of self, a transient perception of an "I."

Following this vast ocean of events, along with countless sequences of other events that could fill entire libraries, here you find yourself in this moment, reading this book. However, for me, my penning down this book is already a distant memory, a reflection in the rearview mirror of time. Currently, as I write this, I'm sitting in the comforts of my home office. It's a beautiful day—a bit grey but beautiful, nonetheless. Mere moments ago, I was getting ready to head to the beach, but a surge of inspiration regarding this chapter kept me tethered to my desk. This very instant, my senses are awash with various stimuli. The subtle aroma of lemongrass wafts from my air diffuser, inexplicably evoking memories of my grandmother. In the distance, I can hear the neighbor mowing his lawn. Each sensory detail, every nuance I perceive in this moment, is the culmination of a myriad of preceding causes. They have coalesced to craft this exact experience. It's a continuum—one event begets another, which sets off a subsequent event, creating a cascade. Before I even realize it, I find myself immersed in the collective outcome of all these interconnected occurrences. And as I dwell in this moment, I am both consciously and unconsciously setting into motion a fresh sequence of events. Simultaneously, countless other chains of events are unfolding, independent of my influence, each contributing to the intricate tapestry of existence. The fact that all of this is happening is truly a miracle. This realization brings a sense of wonderment about the interconnectedness of life and our place within it. It's a reminder that while we may not always see or understand the full picture, we are very much a part of its intricate design. But, now, that thought is already a memory.

Pivoting back to trading, the market is akin to life—we are dealing with an intricate web of variables that influence its continuous dynamics. While we can surely get a general sense of where things are going, pinpointing the exact nuances of short-term variations remains elusive. It's imperative to understand that traders fixated on forecasting every market movement often end up at a disadvantage; they find themselves on the losing end. Perhaps behind that intolerance of the unknown is an existential dread—why are we here? Why do we die? Is there an afterlife? What is the meaning of existence and our place in this vast universe? These profound and timeless questions have propelled humanity to seek answers in patterns and systems since time immemorial. From ancient civilizations drawing patterns in the stars, concocting stories and mythologies to explain celestial events, to our current endeavors in fields like quantum physics, biology, and even artificial intelligence, there's an enduring quest to demystify the universe's machinations. These pursuits often overlap with spirituality and philosophy as we attempt to fathom the meaning and purpose behind the world's intricate design. In financial markets, this manifests as a search for foolproof strategies and patterns that unlock the key to consistent profits. However, much like the philosopher pondering life's existential questions or the astronomer gazing deep into the cosmos, a trader must acknowledge and respect the limits of their understanding.

A mindset overly attached to predictions, especially in regard to trade outcomes, clashes with the very essence of the market, which is, to reiterate, wrapped in layers of uncertainty. Thus, the more a trader finds themselves prone to making errors, feeling the emotional turbulence of market fluctuations, or becoming deeply invested in the outcome of each trade, the more vital it becomes for them to recognize and wholeheartedly accept the omnipresent market uncertainty. It is my hope that this chapter has provided some much-needed perspective on the topic. However, make no mistake:

it's not enough to work with theory. Experience is central to understanding. It's not enough to conceptualize and form theoretical constructs; one must see and feel, through actual experience, why something is true or untrue. One must delve into tangible, visceral experiences to uncover real understanding. One must put their fears and anxieties relating to uncertainty to the test to see whether or not they hold substantive validity. It's not solely about confronting the unknown but immersing oneself in it, allowing the invisible currents of the uncertain to guide, challenge, and ultimately shape your trading identity. If earnestly reflected upon and implemented, the lessons and practical exercises outlined in this chapter will create a solid foundation that will shepherd you toward that identity that gracefully coexists with the pervasive uncertainty. Next, on this journey toward trading composure, we'll turn our attention to disentangling the emotional "knots" that you have built and reinforced over years of mindlessly reacting to uncertainty. We'll tackle this in the chapter ahead.

Chapter 3
Pillar Two: Fostering a Resilient Emotional Core

Composure Amidst Uncertainty

Trading stands alongside some of the most demanding pursuits in life. Think of it akin to peak athleticism, cutting-edge entrepreneurship, or mastering a musical instrument to the point of virtuosity. These arenas all demand not just skill but an impeccable mindset, a psychological edge if you will, to truly rise above the competition and make a mark. In these high-performance endeavors, the mindset isn't just a supplementary factor but a cornerstone of the success equation. Yet, what sets trading apart from these fields is its unique relationship with uncertainty. As an athlete practices a move repeatedly, an entrepreneur strategizes rigorously, and a musician rehearses ardently, each has the power to influence outcomes with a considerable level of predictability. In contrast, a trader has a unique challenge at hand: the ever-shifting landscape that is the market makes it so that past trends and patterns do not always guarantee future results. This higher level of uncertainty demands a strategic approach but also a mental framework finely calibrated to thrive in the face of that inherent ambiguity. This unique mindset, though challenging to maintain, becomes the defining line between fleeting success and sustained excellence in the trading world.

As we've seen in Chapter 2, the first step in developing that mindset is to learn to accept the reality of uncertainty, not just theoretically but also experientially. Uncertainty, in its purest form, is a neutral force. It's neither good nor bad on its own. Hence, the real challenge arises not from uncertainty itself but from the myriad interpretations and meanings we attach to it. When faced with the unknown, our mind often leaps to conclusions, driven by our past experiences, societal conditioning, or even genetic predispositions. It's as though uncertainty becomes a mirror, reflecting our deepest fears, biases, and vulnerabilities. From an evolutionary perspective, uncertainty equates with potential danger, loss, or failure. This makes sense—our ancestors needed to be wary of the unknown for survival, whether that unknown was an unfamiliar rustling in the bushes or an unexpected weather change. However, in our modern era, where physical threats are generally less immediate, this hard-wired caution can sometimes be more of a hindrance than a help. In the world of trading, where substantial financial stakes are involved, a trader's primal instinct to perceive uncertainty as a threat will often lead to hasty, emotion-driven decisions rather than rational, data-driven strategies. However, imagine if we reframed our perception of uncertainty for a moment. What if, instead of seeing it as a looming threat, we viewed it as a door to endless possibilities? After all, the unknown can just as readily lead to adventure, positive transformation, and growth as it can to challenges. The spectrum of potential outcomes is vast, yet we often tether ourselves to a limited, often negative, narrative.

In Chapter 2, we embarked on this critical journey of deepening our understanding of uncertainty, especially in relation to trading. We examined the hows and the whys of market uncertainty. Additionally, we explored the inherent statistical nature of the trading endeavor, acknowledging that it fundamentally operates on probabilities rather than absolute certainties. These key insights made clear the importance of redirecting our attention from short-term outcomes, which are typically riddled with random noise, to long-term results shaped by dependable principles such as the law of averages and the principle of large numbers. These statistical laws suggest that over an extended period and a larger number of trades, our results will tend to align more closely with expected probabilities. Central to this idea is the concept of focusing on trading well in the short term without getting overly fixated on immediate outcomes. By doing so, we cultivate a mindset that values process over sporadic gains. This approach encourages traders to develop strategies that are robust, tested, and aligned with long-term objectives, hence grounding their immediate trading behaviors and actions in sound analysis and process. This shift in focus encourages them to adopt approaches that prioritize long-term stability and consistency over fleeting, short-term gains, thus promoting a perspective that views trading as a cumulative process where the real measure of success is not in individual wins or losses but overall performance over time.

The next step in fostering a mindset that thrives amidst market uncertainty involves minimizing—as much as possible—the emotional frictions that arise as the market performs its chaotic number. While the first step detailed in Chapter 2 certainly contributes to this, it alone is insufficient. To truly disengage from the emotional rollercoaster tied to short-term market fluctuations and trade outcomes, a more profound level of self-reflection and inner work is necessary. Again, let me emphasize a critical point: the issue isn't with uncertainty per se. It's what we think and feel that uncertainty represents, which is the potential negative outcome. And this bends our perceptions because, by nature, we humans have an aversion to outcomes we perceive as negative, or even just less than perfect. Think about the psychological conundrum faced by someone with a high intolerance for uncertainty, especially in trading. On one hand, they have this aversion to the unknown, a deeply rooted discomfort with anything that isn't guaranteed. Then, on the other hand, they are engaging in a domain where uncertainty is the rule, not the exception. Every decision, every move involves uncertainty. This dichotomy can create immense internal conflict that must be addressed if that person wants their trading activities to be profitable and sustainable. Imagine a tight-rope walker who fears heights. Each step is laden with the inherent challenge of balancing and the overwhelming dread of falling. This is a similar scenario. Hence, the way one reconciles their deep-seated anxiety of uncertainty with the chaotic tango of the market is via the active development and cultivation of trading composure.

Now, if you were to do an Internet search on trading psychology, you would be inundated with myriad solutions and expert advice that promise immediate results. Everywhere we turn, we encounter guarantees like, "Do this for instant success" or "Purchase this for immediate results." Particularly in the realm of trading, these promises of shortcuts, hacks, and quick fixes, though tempting, rarely work. They're often peppered with generic, one-size-fits-all tips that, while sounding good on paper, don't necessarily translate to real-world results; they offer fleeting, external remedies to deeply rooted internal challenges. That being said, it's essential to differentiate: there are genuinely commendable content and resources developed by seasoned and knowledgeable professionals in the trading sphere. These aren't what I'm addressing here. My contention is primarily that the more generic trading psychology content has become too prevalent. These tend to merely slap a temporary solution on profound issues—akin to placing a Band-Aid on a gaping wound, hoping it heals.

Here's the dilemma: most traders, especially those with at least a year of experience, internally understand what it takes to be consistent and successful in the market. However, they often find it exceedingly difficult to apply this knowledge in a consistent manner. Knowledge isn't the barrier; application is. Bridging that gap demands more than superficial solutions. What is required is a paradigm shift—an entire reframing of one's thought processes, perceptions, and even experiential understanding of the market and broader life perspectives. That paradigm shift is entirely possible and necessary, but it demands commitment. People tend to drift through life without ever taking a moment for introspection. They become automatons, molded and shaped by external circumstances; they reinforce and perpetuate patterns of thought and behavior, like mindless algorithms. Their lives revolve around a routine cycle of meals, work, sleep, and fleeting entertainment. In this algorithmic, mechanical existence, they pursue short-term desires and urges without truly understanding their nature, questioning their purpose, or even seeing whether these short-term pursuits align with their overarching values. And then, these same people enter the trading arena with that same predisposition. This unexamined mode of living is highly consequential, especially in the unforgiving realm of trading. How can one consistently act in their own best interests when they don't even know why they do what they do? It's practically impossible. Hence, to reiterate, the paradigm shifting work I'm prescribing is entirely necessary.

The mind is akin to clay—it is inherently malleable. In more practical terms, it is trainable, alterable, moldable at any stage of one's life. It is helpful to see the mind as a phenomenon, as a manifestation of processes and reactions, rather than something tangible or definitive. Each fleeting second, this phenomenon called "mind" is rearranging itself, adopting new thoughts and patterns, and discarding old ones. These subtle yet continuous transitions reshape our perspectives, beliefs, thoughts, and feelings. Even though that dynamism is ongoing, we don't typically see or recognize it. This is largely because we're deeply immersed in the immediate experiences that ensnare our attention, much like standing nose-to-bark with a tree, being so close that the vast expanse of the forest beyond remains unnoticed. As you endeavor to build and cultivate composure amidst uncertainty, it's vital to start by recognizing the innate malleability of the mind. Rather than letting the vagaries of chance influence the mind's long-term changes, it's crucial to take an active role in shaping its progression in a way that aligns with your overarching trading goals and aspirations. In the dynamic realm of trading, mere passive participation, fueled by naive optimism that you'll magically get better over time, isn't a strategy for success. Intentional and targeted practice is the key.

A Journey of the Mind

In an ancient village nestled between mountains and dense forests, there lived a young girl named Aaya. Aaya was unlike other children her age; she suffered from a debilitating ailment that caused her intense physical pain. Healers tried to alleviate her suffering with potions and chants; sages journeyed from far and wide, offering wisdom; neighboring tribes sent their most revered shamans, hoping to cast away any dark spirits that might be haunting the young girl. Yet nothing seemed to alleviate her suffering. One particular night, the agony was almost too much to bear, and Aaya yearned for a brief respite, even if it was just a fleeting moment of peace. Tears silently streamed down her face as the weight of her condition bore heavily upon her young heart. But in her anguish, Aaya suddenly experienced a random moment of lucid existential clarity. She became aware of her breathing body for the first time in her life. Each inhalation and exhalation felt distinct, and a profound realization struck her that her body was autonomously maintaining this simple yet profound act even in her dire state. As she became more absorbed in the rhythm of her breath, time seemed to stretch, and every nuance became pronounced: the coolness of the air as it entered her nostrils, its warmth as it departed, and the gentle touch of it against the inner walls of her nose.

Gradually, something remarkable happened: Aaya noticed that her pain, while still there, had receded to the background. With her mind in a calmer and more centered state, she gently directed her attention to this pain that had been consuming her for so long. She noticed that when she didn't label or judge the pain and simply experienced it as it was, it was merely a complex tapestry of sensations, each thread with its own distinct texture and nuance, but not inherently good or bad; not inherently pleasant or painful. What we qualify as pain, discomfort, or even pleasure is neutral at its core if the mind isn't constantly there interpreting what is being felt. But Aaya's realization didn't stop there. She observed that this same principle also held true regarding her thoughts and emotions.

Each emotion and thought was just another thread in the vast tapestry of her consciousness, neither inherently positive nor negative until her mind assigned a value to it. And the same went for anything external.

This little practice of observing the subtleties and nuances of reality and accepting them all as they are provided great relief to Aaya, so much so that she turned it into a habit, practicing whenever and wherever she could. She would tune to her breath at night while laying on her bed; she would also practice anywhere and everywhere, while drawing water from the well for her mother, while playing with her younger brother, while assisting her father with the cattle. Whenever pain returned, she would retreat to her breath, grounding herself in the constant of the present moment. This approach didn't eliminate the pain, but it altered her perception of it. In allowing herself to experience her sensations without being consumed by them, over time, Aaya's relation to the pain changed. Through consistent practice, Aaya eventually reached a stage where she no longer categorized her experiences as "pain" or "suffering"; as a result, her mind gradually stopped lacing the experience with fears, anxieties, or interpretations. To her, pain became merely another sensation, one that she could observe without becoming engulfed in. It was not good or bad; it was just there. By simply observing without trying to change or push the pain away, Aaya realized she could coexist with it. It was a part of her experience but not the entirety of it; she didn't need to be defined by her pain or let it dictate the course of her life. But perhaps more importantly, she now understood that the challenges of her life were just a minuscule part of a grander narrative. By transcending her mind's immediate interpretations and judgments, she had tapped into the universal consciousness, an eternal source of wisdom and tranquility. At times, as Aaya kept practicing, the lines between her physical body and the surrounding space would fade; at times, she felt her consciousness stretch, connecting with something much larger and more expansive; at times, she realized that the very essence that animated her being was the same essence that flowed through the trees outside her window, the birds in the sky, the people in her village, and even the distant stars. In these states, the duality of pain and pleasure, of self and other, of life and death, all melted away. Everything was one; everything was everything; all things were inherently perfect as they were; the concept of time dissolved; everything seemed simultaneously profound yet meaningless. In this seeming contradiction, everything had its place and purpose.

Aaya's commitment to this practice deepened her understanding of life, progressively anchoring in her mind an outstanding depth of insight and wisdom uncommon for someone her age. And while Aaya's story is a creation of my imagination, it might very well echo the origins of the practice of meditation. It's entirely conceivable that the state of mindfulness produced by calmly and nonjudgmentally observing phenomena was discovered by our early ancestors, who were only just emerging from the stone age. Individuals like Aaya must have stumbled upon such a profound state of pure awareness long before it was formalized into what we today call mindfulness. These discoveries might have been shared within small communities or passed down through generations as family wisdom. However, it was Gautama the Buddha, with his profound insights and systematic approach, who managed to make mindfulness accessible to a broader audience. While various forms of meditation have been embedded in numerous ancient cultures, the specific act of mindfulness—a purposeful, nonjudgmental, piercing attentiveness to one's present experience cultivated as part of a structured discipline—is distinctly rooted in Buddhist traditions (Nash 2019). Ancient texts, dating back over 2,500 years, depict the Buddha delineating this framework that went on to transcend regional boundaries and continues to influence millions worldwide.

The Buddha's profound explorations of the psyche delved deep into understanding its underlying mechanisms. The human mind is an intricate tapestry woven with both complexity and startling simplicity. Fundamentally, its operations can be distilled down to two primal instincts: craving and aversion, desire and distaste. These are the polar opposites that dictate much of our behavior. Consider the basic life of a single-celled organism, like a bacterium.

It instinctively gravitates toward conditions fostering its survival and reproduction while retreating from those threatening its existence. Humans, on the surface, might seem vastly different, given the web of our intricate thoughts and emotions. However, at our core, we, too, are governed by this simple push-and-pull mechanism. The innate drive to grow and expand, juxtaposed against the avoidance of entropy and decay, dictates our actions at the most fundamental level. While humans might share the foundational drive with simpler organisms, our evolution has layered on intricacies. We've sculpted our environments, engineered technologies to mitigate life's uncertainties, and instituted societies with structured rules and norms. These collective efforts aim to harmonize our paths, steering us toward a shared vision of the future where we thrive. Unlike animals, driven purely by instincts, our heightened intelligence and consciousness elevate us, granting us the ability to introspect, innovate, and interconnect. However, in situations where the reins of control and predictability elude us, our primordial instincts resurface.

Financial markets serve as a poignant example. Here, even the most seasoned individuals can fall prey to raw, impulsive reactions. Hence, trading is no minor feat, particularly when it's one's livelihood. It demands not just technical skill but also composure and acumen. Immediate whims of the mind often don't align with long-term benefits. In its inherent design, the market ensnares the mindless and impulsive, redistributing their wealth to those who navigate with more profound, analytical insight and judgment. To truly thrive in this domain, a trader must transcend base instincts—the mindless desire and aversion push and pull—and nurture a more profound, insightful, and harmonious mind. And this is where mindfulness comes in and can truly make a difference. There may not be an exact verbatim quote from the Buddha since they have been passed down orally and, later, in written form spanning centuries. However, in the Pali Canon, a written collection of Buddhist teachings in the Theravada tradition, the Buddha is said to impart a simple yet deep understanding of mindfulness. He describes it as being immersed in, absorbed by, and attentive to the present moment. He then explains: *"Body is not self, feelings are not self, perception is not self, mental constructs are not self and consciousness is not self . . . When one sees this one becomes detached from these things, being detached the passions fade, when the passions have faded one is free, and being free one knows one is free"* ("Anatta—Dhamma Wiki," n.d.).

While this passage might appear unimpressive or even unnecessarily esoteric, it conveys the complex depths of Buddha's teachings on maintaining a pure, untainted observation of one's own existence and experiences. My fictional character, Aaya, reached this state and, in doing so, transcended her physical pain and mental disturbances. Without judgment, those were perceived as neutral; they simply existed, devoid of labels as positive or negative. Such a perspective offered Aaya liberation from her habitual patterns of reaction and the tumultuous ebb and flow of her emotions. For traders, harnessing this ability can significantly influence their success rate. This nuanced skill of holding back immediate judgments and impulsive reactions can often be the deciding factor between winning and losing trades, between minimal losses and significant setbacks, and between well-thought-out trades and misguided ones.

Beyond trading, mindfulness has profoundly impacted my own life. As alluded to in the first chapter, I've struggled with a speech impediment for as long as I can remember. More than an occasional misstep in speech, this stutter has erected many obstacles in my path, shaping my interactions and self-perception. Intriguingly, it operates on a cyclical principle: the more I notice it, the deeper my emotional response becomes. This emotional surge, in turn, accentuates the stutter. It's a relentless, self-reinforcing cycle. However, the disciplined application of mindfulness provided me with the agency to disrupt this cycle. In moments where I found myself fumbling over words, when frustration, anger, disappointment, or even anxiety threatened to engulf me, I learned to lean into these feelings with a mindful embrace. It's a practice of "letting things be" as they are, without an ounce of judgment or resistance, preventing the self-feeding, self-reinforcing cycle from gaining further momentum. While the stutter hasn't disappeared entirely—it remains a facet of my life—I've achieved a harmonious coexistence over time. This newfound acceptance essentially severed the feedback loop, which has drastically reduced the stutter as a result. An eerily similar thing happens in trading. Many traders plummet into an emotional maelstrom after the market does something they didn't expect or after encountering an unforeseen loss. There's an innate urge to rectify, to reclaim, to restore, to be made whole again, and not in some distant future. Immediately, in this very moment! This response stemming from the primitive desire or aversion instinct I touched on earlier skews their mental equilibrium. Unbeknownst to them, this imbalance precipitates a slew of irrational thoughts and behaviors, from overriding stop limits to venturing recklessly into disproportionate position sizes.

The crux of the matter is that there exist methods to address these challenges, and, in my experience, mindfulness stands out as the most effective one. However, it's imperative to underscore that mindfulness isn't a panacea or a miraculous elixir to life's multifaceted challenges. Instead, it serves as a guiding beacon, an instrument of recalibration. It offers the invaluable gift of perspective, enabling us to perceive situations through the lens of wisdom and insight. While it may not rewrite the narrative of our challenges, it certainly provides the clarity and resilience to navigate them with greater grace, and in the trading arena, that does make a world of difference.

The Self-Reorganizing Nature of the Mind

As I mentioned previously, the practice of mindfulness has had a profound impact on my life. It has especially helped me with a stutter I've always had. That stutter is still a part of me, but since I've begun practicing mindfulness, I've learned to manage it far better than I ever did in the past. As a result, it has become much less noticeable. I consider myself a work in progress, as this condition isn't something that can be completely eliminated, despite what some self-help gurus might claim. Stuttering is complex and not entirely understood; what's more, it requires ongoing, active management. The improvement I've experienced in this area, though, thanks to mindfulness, is quite remarkable—I'm not usually one to brag, but please allow me to do so this time. That aside, beyond my personal life, mindfulness has also revolutionized my trading. It has been incredibly beneficial for the same reasons it helped with my stutter. Mindfulness assists in undoing mental "knots" or "barriers" that aren't helpful in life. These include difficulties in accepting uncertainty, tolerating discomfort, practicing patience, maintaining consistency, engaging in self-reflection, and cultivating resilience and perspective. A regular mindfulness practice can gradually and positively transform the neural pathways responsible for those states.

To understand how this all works, it is essential to delve into the science of neuroplasticity, which lies at the heart of mindfulness's efficacy. Rest assured, I won't bombard you with complex neuroscientific terms or delve deeply into the intricacies of brain regions and their functions. That is not my area of expertise, and it's probably not what you're looking for. We'll keep our discussion straightforward; my emphasis, rooted in both my professional trading background and my experience in coaching traders to success, will remain grounded in the realm of practical application rather than theoretical abstraction.

To begin with, the term "neuroplasticity" is a fusion of two keywords: "neuron," referring to the nerve cells in the brain interconnected via synapses, and "plasticity," denoting the capacity to be shaped, molded, or altered. Hence, the term neuroplasticity embodies the brain's incredible capacity to not only generate new neural pathways but also to undergo a process of reorganization and adaptation in response to how it is used. Realizing the significance of "in response to how it is being used" is crucial. For example, if your habitual response to trading setbacks is frustration and discouragement, you're essentially strengthening the brain's neural pathways that correlate with these emotions. Meanwhile, the neural networks associated with calmness and composure are less engaged and begin to weaken. Likewise, when you allow emotions such as fear or greed to drive your decisions, you are essentially reinforcing these very mental patterns; you are effectively tightening the specific mental knots of fear, greed, and impulsivity. And the more you engage in the thoughts and behaviors that tighten and reinforce those knots, the more your external results in the market—or, more broadly, in life—will echo these internal obstructions. You might notice a corresponding increase in negative outcomes in your life because that is what you are manifesting. I don't mean this in a metaphysical sense; I mean this in a very practical, tangible one. Constantly generating and dwelling on negative or unproductive thoughts and feelings subtly shifts your perception and decision-making processes. You start to view situations, challenges, and opportunities through a lens of pessimism. This attitude can lead to a self-fulfilling prophecy where you unconsciously make choices that result in outcomes that validate your negative or unrealistic expectations.

In contrast, suppose you were to observe your thoughts and emotions without blindly reacting to them. Suppose you cultivated on purpose, as hard as it is, a mental space that allows for more deliberate and considered responses. Over time, this would lead to a significant transformation in your trading behavior; it would become more difficult to get derailed by a bad day or a losing trade, and it would be easier to stick to your strategy. And that behavioral consistency would directly impact your trading performance. As new, more constructive thought patterns are repeated, the brain physically changes—those pathways associated with patience, discipline, and logical analysis are strengthened, while pathways linked to fear, greed, and impulsivity are weakened. You're deliberately and effectively draining the power from these undesirable patterns, and as a result, they slowly begin to atrophy from a lack of mental energy and focus. By intentionally reshaping your internal mental landscape, you inevitably start to manifest a different external reality. Your interactions, decision-making, and reactions to both the market and life's challenges are now all filtered through this positive, insightful, and balanced mindset, leading to generally more positive outcomes.

An analogy can be very effective in driving home this concept of neural plasticity. Think of the brain as a group of muscles glued together. Just as a bodybuilder might focus on specific muscles during a workout, our daily behaviors and thoughts are like exercises targeting different "brain muscles." Regularly engaging in a particular activity or thought pattern is akin to going to the gym and working out a specific muscle group consistently. Over time, just as muscles grow stronger and more defined with regular exercise, the neural pathways associated with these activities or thoughts in our brain become more robust and efficient, much like how a weight-lifter's biceps become bigger and more defined with regular training. Conversely, neglecting certain activities or thought processes is similar to skipping leg day at the gym. Over time, just as muscles atrophy from underuse, the neural pathways in the brain associated with these neglected activities weaken. This explains why regaining a skill after a lengthy hiatus of not practicing it or recovering a sense of well-being after an extended period of depression can be challenging. The "muscles" in the brain associated with these functions have become weaker from disuse. It also explains why some traders struggle to be profitable even after years in the market and with a winning strategy. They have unwittingly reinforced mental knots or barriers that keep them stuck in a pattern of inconsistency. Even when they seem to have periods of consistency in the market, they somehow find a way to veer off course, yet again, perpetually trapped in a cycle of gaining and losing consistency. Their trading journey becomes a repetitive loop of falling off and clambering back onto the "consistency bandwagon."

In my view, one of the most captivating elements of neuroplasticity lies in the brain's remarkable capacity to create new neural connections and pathways. It's akin to the idea that by exercising a specific muscle, you could not only strengthen it but also develop entirely new muscles. While this concept defies the principles of physical muscle development, it's a fascinating reality in the cerebral landscape. When we encounter new challenges or embark on learning new skills, our brain doesn't just enhance the existing neural pathways; it has the astonishing ability to forge entirely new ones.

This adaptability and capability of the brain to rewire and evolve underscores its incredible versatility and strength. Whether mastering a novel skill, adapting to an unfamiliar situation, or healing from psychological trauma, the brain demonstrates an extraordinary capacity for change and growth. The brain's ability to continuously adapt, morph, and expand in response to its experiences and how it is being used is the essence of neuroplasticity. In essence, neuroplasticity is not just a scientific fact; it's a beacon of hope and a testament to the limitless potential of the human mind no matter at what stage it is.

Turning our focus back to mindfulness, understanding its connection with neuroplasticity is vital. Market uncertainty creates a fertile ground for impulsive reactions and emotional decision-making; hence, by intentionally focusing on positive behaviors and thought patterns, we can actively rewire our brains toward patterns of perceptions and behaviors more aligned with our trading goals. However, since awareness is the first step in purposeful neuroplastic change, through the active development of their "mindfulness muscle," traders can enhance their awareness and control over their mental and emotional states. As they become more mindful, their self-regulation skills go through the roof, setting off a cascading effect: the brain slowly restructures itself to support other positive characteristics essential for trading success, like the capacity for insight and the ability to make sharper decisions. In other words, they can better recognize when they're about to make decisions based solely on fear or greed. Instead of succumbing to impulsive reactions, they can consciously choose to pause in these critical moments. This pause allows for a shift from an emotionally charged response to one that is more rational and in alignment with their long-term objectives and strategies. When decisions are repeatedly made based on logical analysis rather than knee-jerk reactions to market changes, mastery matures, and excellence naturally ensues. This is how one takes active control of the process of neuroplasticity; this is how one actively sculpts their brain's neural landscape. Rewiring your brain on purpose isn't a trivial matter; it's a transformative process that can lead to significant personal growth and development. It is how I managed to gain control over my stutter; it is also the approach that revolutionized my trading psychology. This is a journey of understanding your triggers and ongoingly changing your relationship with your emotions so they don't spiral out of control, creating mental knots and compulsive behaviors.

It is crucial to emphasize this point again: Our repeated behaviors and thought processes shape our identity and abilities, for better or worse. Each decision one makes, or defaults to, each thought one entertains, and each action one performs, in and out of the market, reinforce the neural networks in the brain responsible for those experiences. And the more this happens, the stronger and more developed these neural networks become. In the meantime, the patterns in the mind that receive less attention and use shrink and weaken. This concept isn't just theoretical—it has profound practical implications. Most individuals go through life while allowing the whims of fate to dictate their mental state, not realizing their power in shaping their minds and the outcomes they broadly get in life. Yet, this understanding is crucial for traders and anyone looking to lead a fulfilling and intentional life: Every moment offers an opportunity to reinforce positive neural pathways or inadvertently strengthen negative ones. While you might not be in direct control of what happens to you in life, you can directly alter how you respond. And how you respond is everything! You can use what life hands you and paint a vibrant picture, turning challenges into opportunities for growth and learning. Alternatively, you can let life circumstances dictate a bleak narrative, reinforcing negative patterns and perceptions. The choice is akin to selecting the colors for your life's canvas. Opting for bright, positive hues allows you to craft a life story filled with perseverance, adaptation, and progress. In contrast, darker shades might lead to a narrative dominated by pessimism and stagnation. I'm not implying that this process is straightforward or effortless by any means; it's a challenging path, but it yields immensely rewarding outcomes.

Where You Are, There You Are

As a mindfulness instructor, my preferred approach to introducing people to the practice is experiential rather than theoretical. I believe that practice and experience are the best teacher; hence, rather than just discussing the concept of mindfulness endlessly, I like to encourage people to join me in a brief practice session. This way, they can directly experience and understand mindfulness, not merely in an intellectual or theoretical sense, but in a deep, experiential manner. So, let's give it a go. Make yourself comfortable, and just be right where you are.

As you read this sentence, I invite you to engage in an exercise of heightened awareness. If you've found yourself rapidly skimming through the pages of this book, slow down your pace. Take a moment to ease off the urge to rush through the text. Instead, allow yourself to engage more deeply with each word. Savor the nuances of the language, the structure of the sentences, and the rhythm of the narrative.

As your eyes move across this text, become aware of the spaces between the words and sentences and how they all weave together to form meaning.

Feel the weight of the book or the device in your hands, the texture of the pages, or the screen under your fingers. Notice how your eyes move across the text, how your neck and shoulders are positioned, and how it feels to be where you are.

Broaden your focus to include every other element that enters your field of perception—the thoughts in your mind, the rhythm of your breathing, the subtle sensations coursing through your body, the array of sounds permeating your surroundings.

Immerse yourself in this moment as it is currently unfolding. Allow your mind to be fully present with what is.

Embrace a holistic sense of being in this moment. You are existing in a dynamic environment, with a multitude of experiences coinciding. Allow yourself to be present with all of it, the seen and the unseen, the heard and the unheard, the felt and the unfelt.

Take a few moments to linger on that last sentence. Let it resonate within you. Approach it with an open, nonjudgmental mindset. There is no need to categorize it as good or bad, right or wrong. Simply be present with the words and the impact they have on you. Let the sentence exist as it is, as a series of words with a unique vibration and significance.

Observe any reactions or emotions that are surfacing. Pay particular attention to your thoughts. Notice if your thoughts are racing or wandering or are calm and focused. Are they positive, negative, or neutral? This observation isn't about judging your thoughts but about becoming aware of their nature and flow.

Next, let go of any conceptual or structured thoughts and simply be. Close your eyes and take a few moments to do this.

If you're reading these words, your eyes are now open. And they're open because you had a conscious or unconscious thought or urge to open them. That's perfectly fine, but let us try again. When you find your mind wandering to what you should be doing next, what you could be experiencing instead, or what you ate for lunch yesterday, gently acknowledge these thoughts and then let them fade into the background. Then, return your focus to the here and now, to the act of simply existing in the present. Letting go requires no effort; it merely requires mindful awareness and acceptance. Close your eyes again for a few breaths, a brief span of seconds, or a few minutes.

Previously, before you started this exercise, you were probably glancing over the words and speed reading, but now you are more present and deliberate. Keep that pace, and notice the words, how each letter and word is formed, and the space between them. Notice how understanding is occurring effortlessly. Notice how instinctual cognizing and information processing are.

Become an observer of your own experience, witnessing without judgment or analysis. This practice of heightened awareness, even briefly, is a glimpse into the essence of mindfulness—being fully and consciously present in the here and now.

Notice the rhythm of your breathing. Notice the rise and fall of your chest or abdomen. Feel the air moving in and out of your nostrils or mouth. Observe these sensations without trying to alter them, simply allowing your breath to flow naturally.

Notice the subtle sensations in your body. Feel the weight of your body on the chair or the ground. Notice any areas of tension or relaxation. Be aware of the temperature of the air on your skin and the feeling of your clothes against your body. Acknowledge discomfort or comfort, but try not to judge or change what is being felt. Just observe.

Expand your awareness to sounds around you. Listen to the various noises that fill your environment. It could be the distant hum of traffic, the ticking of a clock, or more immediate sounds like your own breathing. Recognize each sound without getting attached to it or thinking about its source.

As always, maintain a gentle, nonjudgmental attitude. If your mind gets carried away by thoughts, which is natural, simply notice the distraction and then kindly redirect your attention back to the present exercise.

Remember, the goal is not to empty your mind of thoughts but to be aware of each moment, accepting it as it is.

Once more, gently close your eyes after reading this final piece of guidance. Settle into a sense of gratitude for the way things inherently exist, embracing both the external environment and your internal world as they are. Try not to engage in any analytical thought processes; simply embrace this reality: things are as they are, and in their own way, they are perfectly so. Do this for a few cycles of breath, a few brief moments, or even a few minutes.

Looking Within or Beyond—A Time for Both

In the previous exercise, you likely accessed some level of mindful awareness. Depending on how busy your mind was, the quality of mindful awareness might have ranged from a fragmented state to a more steady, uninterrupted flow. This variability is completely normal and expected, especially for those new to the practice. As you make mindfulness a daily habit, you may find that your ability to maintain a continuous stream of mindful awareness improves. Think of it as akin to muscle strengthening, mastering a musical instrument, or refining your trading skills: the more regular and dedicated your practice, the more proficient you become.

The simplicity of the instructions is something you might also have noticed. Whether you are sitting, standing, or in another posture, whether your eyes are open or closed, the essence of the practice remains the same. It's about taking a moment to become acutely aware of your current experiences, observing them without judgment, with full acceptance of what is as it is. There are many meditation resources nowadays, each offering different methods and techniques. These resources range from straightforward and beginner-friendly to more complex and advanced practices. However, at the core, mindfulness's essence is simply unconditional, unadulterated presence, and based on my experience, the most effective approach to it strikes a balance between simplicity and depth. Moreover, trading is a unique endeavor with specific challenges; hence, tailored mindfulness strategies are necessary for effectively navigating the market's tumultuous terrain. Understanding the distinct needs of traders, my team and I have crafted a comprehensive series of mindfulness practices specifically designed to fit the realities of trading. These meditations, which I've been offering on my website for several years, are structured to assist traders in navigating the highs and lows of the market while maintaining mental clarity and composure. The feedback has been overwhelmingly positive, with numerous individuals expressing how these meditations have significantly aided their trading journey. But, whether you explore the meditation resources provided by my team or learn from other meditation teachers and platforms, it's crucial to dedicate time every day to this practice. It is equally vital to integrate it into your everyday life, off the meditation cushion.

One other essential point that is often left out in most meditation resources is the importance of selecting a meditation style that resonates with your personality, current emotional state, or particular challenges you're facing at the moment. In that regard, there are two main styles of meditation to choose from: inward-focused meditations and outward-focused meditations. Inward-focused meditations, as the name implies, revolve around directing your attention inward to your internal state. This could involve closing your eyes and zooming in on your breathing, noticing the subtle sensations within your body, or being aware of your thoughts and emotions. In essence, the reason to engage in this type of meditation is to cultivate and strengthen your awareness of your internal state, which can be crucial for managing emotions, reducing stress, and enhancing self-awareness. In the high-stakes world of trading, such a heightened level of self-awareness can mean the difference between a trade managed with emotions and one managed with reason. Outward-focused meditation, in contrast, involves anchoring your attention to the external environment. This might include focusing on a specific object, paying attention to the sounds around you, or simply observing the world with a quiet, nonjudgmental awareness. This practice benefits people who may get too caught up in their internal thoughts and emotions, leading to heightened stress or a skewed perspective. By shifting focus to the external world, you can find a grounding balance, helping to maintain stability amidst internal turmoil. This type of meditation can be particularly helpful for traders who find themselves overwhelmed by the rapid pace and constant fluctuations of the market. It allows them to step back, gain perspective, and interact with the market in a more objective and less emotionally charged way. Outward-focused meditation encourages a broader view of the situation, fostering a sense of calm and collectedness that can be invaluable in making sound trading decisions.

When deciding which meditation style to adopt, reflecting on your natural disposition is important. Are you generally more inward-focused or outward-focused? A straightforward way to gauge this is by conducting a simple exercise: close your eyes and pay attention to what naturally draws your focus. Do you immediately tune into your internal sensations, thoughts, and emotions? Moreover, do you feel them acutely? Or do you notice your mind wandering toward external sounds, sensations, and environmental stimuli? This exercise can reveal your natural propensity for inward or outward focus. If you have an inherent inward focus, outward-focused meditation practices can help you deepen your connection with and awareness of the world around you, balancing your natural tendency. If you have an inherent outward focus, inward-focused meditation practices might enhance your introspective abilities and emotional self-awareness. Again, it's all about balance. Additionally, the aim is not to categorize one state or practice as better than the other but to understand your natural inclination so you can choose a meditation practice that best supports your current needs, especially considering the unique demands of trading.

After you've determined your meditation style based on your natural tendency, it's also crucial to determine which meditation is better given the situation you currently find yourself in. For instance, regardless of where you are on the inward-outward continuum, if you're feeling anxious on a particular day, that anxiety might get exacerbated if you were to do an inward-focused meditation as it would likely heighten the experience of your internal state. Instead, try an outward-focused meditation to take your attention off your uncomfortable internal state. By keeping your eyes open and focusing on a fixed point in front of you (for instance), you can anchor your attention outside yourself, easing the undue focus on your internal happenings. I want to emphasize that both states and practices are integral to a well-rounded mindset, where internal intuition and understanding are balanced with external insight, leading to better life outcomes overall.

There are meditations that are designed to balance inward and outward awareness simultaneously, and the one we practiced previously did just that. However, it is crucial to recognize when to emphasize one over the other, as there will be times when you need to specifically target one area to align with your immediate needs. For example, an inward-focused meditation might be more beneficial if you are overwhelmed by market stress or personal concerns. It allows you to delve into your thoughts and emotions, offering a deeper understanding and a chance to find internal peace amidst chaos. On the other hand, if you're feeling disconnected from your environment or too absorbed in your thoughts, an outward-focused meditation can help ground you in the present moment and reconnect you with the world around you. The key is to be aware, adaptive, and responsive to your current needs.

Sustaining Composure Through S.T.A.Y

Picture this scenario: Your day begins with a morning meditation, setting a serene and balanced tone as you prepare to start trading. You're feeling calm and collected, going through your pre-trading routine—checking futures, catching up on the latest news, and reviewing your action plan. The market opens, and you patiently wait for the right moment to make your move. Everything seems to be going smoothly. However, the market takes a downturn not long after, and you face your first loss of the day. Your calm demeanor is shaken but not shattered. You manage to keep it together, and with resilience, you bide your time for the next viable trade. When this opportunity arises, you make your move, the market wiggles around a bit, and goes on to tickle your profit target, only to wind back down and hit your stop loss—again! Your frustration and annoyance are now brimming under the surface, and the peace and equanimity you had earlier are now hanging by a thread. Determined to recoup your losses, you enter another trade, however, this time with increased stakes. Unfortunately, fortune does not favor you that day, and this trade, too, results in a loss. Your tranquility and balance are now completely gone, and you end the trading session feeling defeated. You feel overwhelmed not only by the financial loss but also by the realization that you've strayed from your trading rules, allowing your emotions to take control. This is an all-too-common experience for traders. Hence, the real test of your mindfulness practice isn't during the calm moments on the meditation cushion; it's how you apply these principles in your daily life, especially in adverse situations. What is the point of attaining calmness, focus, and centeredness during meditation if you abandon that equilibrium as soon as the practice ends? If mindfulness is discarded at the first signs of trouble, it won't be of much help in overcoming the challenges of trading.

A common adage in meditation communities is "practice is circular." This phrase can be interpreted in several ways. Firstly, the notion refers to the importance of returning to the basics. Just as a circle has no beginning or end, mindfulness continually brings us back to fundamental principles, no matter how advanced one becomes. It's a reminder that, at its core, mindfulness is about being present in the moment and that this simple truth remains constant regardless of how far you progress in your practice. Another meaning of the saying "practice is circular" is the idea that practice does not exist in isolation but as part of a larger cycle that includes every aspect of one's daily life. The skills and awareness you cultivate during mindfulness meditation are meant to flow seamlessly into your daily activities, influencing how you respond to stress, make decisions, and interact with others. Lastly, the idea that "practice is circular" implies that the benefits of mindfulness reinforce and enhance the practice itself. As you apply mindfulness in real-life situations, the insights and improvements you experience feed back into your meditation practice, deepening your understanding and skill. This creates a positive feedback loop where practice informs life, and life, in turn, enriches practice.

Many traders find themselves being dictated not so much by the market but by their emotional reactions to it. They feel elated if their positions are doing well; if not, they plunge into despair. Their mood swings wildly with the market because they haven't learned to detach their emotional well-being from market fluctuations. Hence, when incorporating mindfulness into one's daily regimen, the key is to understand that practice is circular and that mindfulness needs to be maintained throughout the day. By consistently seeking to be mindful while eating, walking, showering, resting, as well as in high-stakes activities like trading, you gradually cultivate steadiness of mind. This steady state allows you to observe events and circumstances with detachment, reducing the likelihood of emotional volatility. Of course, it is not easy to remember to be mindful. The day-to-day demands of a busy life can easily sweep away our best intentions. This is why a structured and dedicated approach to mindfulness is crucial. When practice remains at the forefront of one's mind, cultivating an automatic response of mindfulness to stressors and challenges becomes almost instinctive.

As with the mnemonic F.A.C.E. presented in Chapter 2, I've encapsulated some key guidelines into a new mnemonic to help you weave mindfulness into the fabric of your daily life. This new mnemonic, named S.T.A.Y., is intended to facilitate the emergence of mindfulness, thus creating a buffer between you and the immediate reactions to the ups and downs of life or the market. S.T.A.Y. conveys the idea of grounding oneself entirely in the present moment, upholding an undistracted state of awareness, and "staying" with unfolding experience as it is while refraining from any judgments or diversions. As you get better at "staying," the circularity of practice will establish itself: your mood will stabilize, your reasoning will be more thoughtful and deliberate, you'll regulate your emotions more easily, and as a result, the outcomes you experience will be increasingly positive.

As a mnemonic, S.T.A.Y. stands for:

- S: Start and End Your Day with Meditation
- T: Take Time for Self-Reflection
- A: Active Acceptance of Uncertainty
- Y: Yield to the Trading Process

Let's explore each step individually:

S: Start and End Your Day with Meditation

My mornings are sacred, a carefully crafted prelude to the high-stakes conditions of trading. They begin in the still, predawn hours at precisely 5:00 a.m. There is a unique serenity in these early hours, a quietude that the world has yet to disturb. In these moments, as the darkness gently recedes, my mind is at its most receptive, open to deep reflection and meditation; therefore, engaging in a 20-to-30-minute meditation session as the first act of the day is not merely a routine, it's the first step in my deliberate practice of grounding myself in a state of mindfulness.

Similar to my mornings, my evenings too are sacred—right before bed, I offer myself another gift of meditation. This helps me unwind and prepare my mind for a restful night's sleep. There is no need to maintain a sitting posture for this session; I simply lie in bed just before drifting into slumber and allocate 20 to 30 minutes to observe my inner world. Although the day's events may naturally surface in my mind, rather than immersing myself in them, I approach them with a sense of detachment, as a scientist observing phenomena. As thoughts or feelings arise, I embrace them without passing judgment, allowing them to come and go gently. During this evening meditation, I also have the opportunity to express gratitude for the day's experiences, regardless of their nature. It's perfectly acceptable to feel disheartened when faced with adverse events in trading. However, it's equally crucial to keep the broader context of one's life in mind. Remember that challenging moments provide valuable lessons about what works and what doesn't, foster a deeper appreciation for the positive aspects of life, and contribute to the rich tapestry of complexity and intrigue that makes life so fascinating. In a world devoid of challenges, we become feeble, and life becomes dull and unremarkable. During the session, I deliberately bring this to mind.

Meditation can seem dull to many. In an age where idle moments are often filled with smartphone scrolling, sitting in silence and focusing on the breath can be challenging for a restless mind. It is likely to resist this new, quieter mode of being. Therefore, whatever your preferred meditation style or practice may be, the most crucial element is to go about it strategically, or else you'll do it once or twice and quickly fall off the bandwagon. This is where a technique called "Don't Break the Chain" can be helpful. Here's how it works: get yourself a yearlong calendar, preferably one you can display prominently or keep within easy view on your desk. Then, simply mark off each day you meditate, creating a visual chain of your commitment. The beauty of this approach lies in the visual reinforcement it provides; watching your chain of successes grow day by day becomes a motivational tool in itself (see Figure 3.1).

Su	Mo	Tu	We	Th	Fr	Sa
1	2	3	4	5	6	7
8	9	10	11	12	13	14
15	16	17	18	19	20	21
22	23	24	25	26	27	28
29	30	31				

Figure 3.1 "Don't Break the Chain" calendar—A visual commitment to meditation.

This strategy taps into several psychological principles. Firstly, the act of marking your calendar triggers a dopamine release in the brain, similar to the satisfaction derived from ticking off a to-do list. This dopamine rush reinforces the habit, creating a positive feedback loop. Moreover, the "Don't Break the Chain" method helps mitigate the "Just This Once" mindset, which often derails habit formation. "Just this once, I won't meditate." With a visual reminder of your progress, you won't easily fall for such short-term urges. Your resolve will likely stand firm (see Figure 3.2).

Another aspect this method leverages is the psychological principle of "loss aversion," where the pain of losing is more compelling than the pleasure of gaining. The thought of breaking a long streak of consistency becomes a powerful motivator to continue, tapping into our innate desire to avoid loss and regret.

This "don't break the chain" method is often attributed to Jerry Seinfeld, the famous comedian, actor, writer, and producer; however, in actuality, it is rooted in age-old practices. I vividly recall my grade schoolteacher using a similar approach to help us build consistency in our daily assignments. The method works so well because it is a formidable habit-forming tool that leverages the

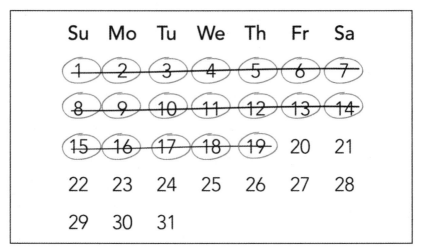

Figure 3.2 A calendar marked with daily meditation sessions embodying the "Don't Break the Chain" technique. The growing chain of marked days serves not only as a record of progress but also as a powerful motivator to sustain the practice.

intricate interplay of our brain's reward and loss systems to keep us on track. Remarkably, its versatility extends beyond habits like meditation and can be effectively applied in contexts such as trading. For instance, one can mark the days where they perfectly adhered to their trading rules, regardless of outcomes, thereby bolstering the commitment to maintain a consistent trading pattern.

Irrespective of the habit you endeavor to nurture, it is crucial to bear in mind that occasional slip-ups are acceptable. What matters is not letting one lapse halt your progress. Should a break of the chain occur, simply resume without connecting the missed day, maintaining an accurate record of your journey. At the end of the day, consistency is how you make anything stick. In the case of meditation, as the habit solidifies, the initial resistance of the mind diminishes, and the once daunting task of sitting in stillness becomes a source of peace and rejuvenation. Consistency also allows you to gradually notice the subtle changes in your mental and emotional landscape, reinforcing the value of the practice and motivating you to continue.

T: Take Time for Self-Reflection

By the time my morning meditation session concludes, around 6:00 a.m. at the latest, I am mentally and emotionally ready to face the day's challenges with clarity and composure. But the mental preparation doesn't end here. As my partner wakes and begins preparing breakfast, our day continues with a unique and cherished ritual that has become a cornerstone of our relationship—mutual, contemplative silence. This shared practice is far from being a void; it's a canvas for further introspection and reflection. In this tranquil environment, my thoughts have the freedom to breathe and wander, allowing me to explore the vast landscapes of my mind. This silent communion with myself is crucial as it enables me to conduct an internal assessment of my feelings and thoughts. How am I feeling as I begin this new trading day? What is on my mind, and what emotional undercurrents are present? Am I harboring any lingering anxieties or stresses that could affect my trading decisions? How are my energy levels, and what can I do to optimize them? Is there a particular aspect of my trading plan that needs more focus or revision? What lessons did I learn from yesterday's trading session, and how can they be applied today? How can I better manage my emotions during the highs and lows of the market? Are there any biases influencing my decision-making process that I need to be aware of? How can I maintain my composure and stay true to my strategy, even under pressure? This intentional inner dialogue is an important step in aligning my emotional and mental state with the day's requirements; it offers an opportunity to pay attention to where my mind is, to recalibrate, or to take the day off if needed.

Now, you might wonder, "Isn't this what we do during meditation?" Not exactly. The distinction between reflection and meditation is crucial: meditation involves a deep, intentional release of thought and emotional patterns, whether structured or not. We're fostering a state of mindful presence. On the other hand, reflection engages the mind more actively. We use our thoughts and intellect to ponder, analyze, and derive insights from our experiences and emotions. It's a process of engaging with our thoughts to understand and learn rather than letting them go as we do in meditation. This active engagement with our thoughts during reflection allows us to gain clarity, solve problems, and enhance our self-awareness, complementing the mindful state cultivated in meditation. I trust this distinction is now more apparent. But whether we're talking about one or the other, most traders have no such grounding morning rituals. They often bypass introspection and self-assessment, thinking that market analysis and strategy planning alone are sufficient for success. In an ideal world, they are, but in reality, the human mind is susceptible to emotional and psychological influences that can significantly impact trading decisions and subsequent outcomes.

In my experience coaching hundreds of traders toward success, I've observed a significant pattern: those who lead an examined life and are intentional about how they approach their trading days consistently outperform those who don't in the market. While the outperformers' morning rituals won't precisely mirror mine, the key element they share is dedicated time for self-reflection and mental preparation. These traders understand the importance of aligning their mental state with the day's trading activities. They might engage in a combination of different practices, such as light exercise and journaling or meditation, followed by reading something inspirational. Still, the essence remains the same—a deliberate effort to center themselves before facing the market. This introspective approach helps them develop a level of self-awareness that is critical in managing the emotional highs and lows of trading. They become adept at recognizing their emotional triggers and biases, allowing for more rational and objective decision-making. It's not just about preparing for the market's technical challenges but also about equipping themselves to handle the psychological demands of trading. Moreover, this practice of starting the day with a focus on introspection contributes to building a growth mindset. These traders are more open to learning from their positive and negative experiences, as they understand that trading is not just a skill to be mastered but a continuous journey of personal development.

A: Active Acceptance of Uncertainty

Every day, as you sit down to trade, you must carry with you not just a well-prepared strategy but also a mind that aligns with the realities of the market. Most traders, at the bottom, are inconsistent because they live their lives based on their emotions. This isn't to say that emotions are bad. Emotions are a vital part of the human experience, but they often lead to detrimental outcomes in trading. Emotions are powerful and can vividly color our experiences, leading to trading decisions based on momentary feelings—being disciplined and consistent when things feel right and easy and stopping when motivation wanes or challenges arise. The key to breaking this cycle is developing the capacity to maintain a steady, purposeful mindset amidst the fluctuating scenarios of trading and life. And that constancy starts by heeding a crucial insight we've discussed: Any trade can be a loser no matter how large your edge is. Welcome to uncertainty!

Your emotional trading decisions stem from a discomfort with uncertainty. Now, it's important to remember that embracing uncertainty won't come easily and naturally. It is crucial to recognize that it is a gradual process and will take time. Having said that, you should take active control of the process of rewiring your brain to embrace uncertainty instead of leaving it up to the vagaries of chance. This cannot be emphasized enough. Odds are that you've already recognized some of the emotional and physical responses that uncertainty can trigger within you. Sweaty hands, a knot in your stomach, and racing thoughts are all common reactions. These responses are part of our innate fight-or-flight mechanism, designed to help us navigate potentially dangerous situations. However, these physical and emotional reactions can be counterproductive in many modern circumstances, such as trading. The trick to alleviating such reactions is consciously making it an intention to challenge our intolerance of uncertainty. When you notice your usual physical and emotional reactions to uncertainty, double down on the adherence to your trading rules, irrespective of your emotions and catastrophizing thoughts.

Typically, if you're struggling with consistency, I recommend trading with small sizes to make things easier on you. Show up, take your trades, and tell yourself that, win or lose, you need that experience to grow into the trader you're meant to become. Allow the numbers to play out and observe the outcome across numerous trades. If your trading strategy or system is viable probabilistically and statistically, you will notice favorable outcomes despite the looming uncertainty, which will slowly shift your perspective on uncertainty. There comes a point when it will no longer be a source of fear or anxiety because you'll know, through experience, how that uncertainty eventually resolves itself. But the key word here is "slowly." Most traders are right away attempting to make a lot of money fast without having developed the self-mastery needed to accomplish this goal, which is entirely counterproductive.

An additional step, tangentially linked to the previous one, to help mitigate emotional responses in trading and shorten your path to your grand trading goal is to constantly remind yourself of the factors that are within your control. A comprehensive examination of life reveals that certain aspects are more and less under our control. Consider your possessions, interpersonal relationships, place of birth, ethnicity, the people you encounter, their thoughts, the weather, market fluctuations, the outcomes of your trades—all these external factors, and others, in reality, are subject to your control to a lesser degree than you might assume. In some instances, you may have no control over them whatsoever. Conversely, your own beliefs, the thoughts you deliberately entertain, your perception of reality, your desires, aversions, and ultimately, your actions are areas where you possess more substantial control.

In my coaching practice, I often advise students to create a table that distinguishes between elements within their direct control and those beyond it (see Table 3.1). On one side, we have factors that fall under their direct control, such as entry and exit points, risk management protocols, and their own behavior. These aspects are malleable, allowing for adjustments, refinement, and optimization to enhance overall trading performance. Conversely, on the other side of the table, we find elements outside their direct control, such as geopolitical events, economic data releases, market participants' emotions, and their impact on market prices. Regardless of one's

Table 3.1   A visual representation of what is within or beyond our control

Within My Direct Control	Beyond My Direct Control
Entry and exit points	Geopolitical events
Risk management protocols	Economic data releases
My own behavior	Market participants' emotions

skill or experience, these external variables are difficult to predict and manage with reliable accuracy, especially on the retail end.

By drawing the table, this visual aid and potent reminder, and placing it on their desk, my students are better able to see the controllable and uncontrollable aspects of trading. As a result, they can better manage themselves and their emotions. We have more power than we realize; it's just that we often misdirect that power toward things we have little control over instead of focusing on what we can control.

Beyond human perception, reality is largely neutral, with occurrences unfolding through a chain of impersonal causes and effects. Understanding and consistently reinforcing this concept in your mind grants you significant control over your life. For instance, during challenging times, such as a series of trading losses, discerning the elements within your control can alleviate unnecessary concerns regarding things you once believed were subject to your influence. Realizing that you can modify your perspective empowers you to view and experience the situation more positively. The moment you shift from attempting to control and predict market outcomes to focusing on adapting your internal thought patterns and behaviors to align with how the market distributes profits, you position yourself more favorably. By understanding and working with the market's dynamics and the reality of uncertainty rather than against them, you set the stage for profitable opportunities. This approach improves your trading results and brings about more positive outcomes in your life overall.

Y: Yield to the Trading Process

Losses are an inextricable element of the trading process. When you trade, you will have losses. As a trader, it is essential to acknowledge that this is not a question of "if" but "when." Furthermore, it's worth noting that, at times, these losses will come in clusters. If that doesn't make you profoundly humble, then I don't know what can. And if you have no humility, you can't do well as a trader.

The struggle most people experience in trading stems from the deep-rooted aversion to uncertainty. They repudiate it; they pretend it's not there or overly stress about it. This is primarily due to uncertainty's intricate link to the idea of loss. And who likes losses? Of course, nobody does. But losses in trading are not like any other losses; they're stepping-stones on one's path to their grand trading goals. This is particularly true for systematic losses, which occur when traders adhere to their established trading rules. Consider the process of scientific investigation, a foundation of human progress. In scientific experiments, a multitude of results, both positive and negative, are generated, each serving as a valuable data point. Scientists do not perceive failures as setbacks but rather as essential data points that contribute to their understanding of the thing they're trying to understand. Trading also requires such a detached approach; trading requires us to yield to its inherent process. Just as scientists embrace failures as essential components of their research, traders must accept losses as part of their journey. Every trade, whether it results in a profit or a loss, is a data point—merely that, nothing more, nothing less. And that data point contributes to our understanding of ourselves, our strategies, and the market.

I vividly recall a moment during a meditation retreat in British Columbia, Canada, that contributed to my experiential understanding of yielding and surrendering to the process, offering valuable insights into my challenges in trading. During the retreat, in the cozy seclusion of my meditation tent, I found myself confronted by an unexpected visitor. As I sat cross-legged, eyes closed and engrossed in the contemplation of my inner landscape, I was suddenly jolted by a sensation of movement on my leg. Deliberately, I eased my eyes open, only to discover a sizable spider steadily ascending my lap. Since I've always harbored an irrational fear of arachnids, my initial reaction was to panic. I hastily stood up and tossed the spider out using my flip-flops while trying not to harm it. With the spider safely beyond the threshold, I returned to my meditation practice, trying to re-center myself in the present moment. However, fate had a different plan, as moments later, I opened my eyes again to a sight that left me horrified—the spider had returned, perched once again on my lap. This time, I impulsively sent it flying with a swift flick, hoping this would end our encounter. However, it returned not once but twice more, each time making its way back to my lap during meditation. It was as though the spider was determined to teach me a lesson.

By the fourth encounter, my irrational fear had transformed into a sense of mindful acceptance. I took a deep, calming breath and consciously observed the spider's presence without succumbing to the torrent of thoughts and fears that had previously gripped me. Within me was a whirlwind of thoughts and emotions—fear, apprehension, the instinct to control the situation—all surging like waves in my consciousness. However, I surrendered, somehow, fully embracing the reality of the situation—"A spider is settling on my lap...so what?" I let go of the need to act or react, allowing the moment to play out organically. "Are you trying to teach me something?" I silently whispered to the eight-legged visitor, half-expecting a response. Of course, the spider remained silent, but its presence felt strangely captivating. I closed my eyes and felt it continuing its slow, deliberate climb, almost as if it were going for my exposed neck and face. I felt my old patterns of fear urging me to react, but my resolve was firm, and I stayed. As I focused on my breath and viscerally accepted the experience as it was, I began to feel a profound sense of connection with all living beings, including this arachnid companion. Seconds turned into minutes, and minutes turned into almost two hours, and the retreat's bell eventually signaled the end of our meditation session. I slowly opened my eyes, and to my surprise, my friend had disappeared. It was as though it had completed its mission, leaving me with a newfound understanding of myself.

This experience may seem like an ordinary encounter blown out of proportion. However, it had a lasting impact on me, acting as a powerful reminder that our greatest teachers often appear in unexpected forms. The things we fear are often precisely what we need to stay with and surrender to. In trading, how often do we encounter unexpected challenges, uncertainties, or losses? And how frequently do we respond with an instinctual panic, desperately trying to shake off the discomfort they bring and make matters worse? By choosing to observe without attachment, with complete surrender toward what is, we gradually de-energize our catastrophizing thoughts. We realize that thoughts and emotions, much like the spider itself, are transient, no matter their intensity. They come and go, just as the ebbs and flows of the market. In understanding this, we release our grip on them, realizing that the more we hold on, the stronger they become and the longer they persist. As we refrain from struggling against our fears and discomforts, we avoid getting trapped in a mindset that conflicts with how the market distributes profits.

Trading need not be complicated. Often, we complicate it unnecessarily by working it up in our minds. We are fixated on the wins; we agonize over the losses; we resist the uncertainties. But what if we intentionally simplified our mental approach? What if we let go of wanting immediate results, instead yielding to the peak and valley process, gradually leading to positive aggregate results? As someone who has made this mental transition, it's the key to ensuring that trading remains profitable and sustainable. Remember, emotions and money are like oil and water; they don't mix well. Therefore, keep your emotions out of trading. Do your best. Your success depends on it.

* * *

Imagine this scenario: You've done your homework and have a solid action plan for the trading day. You've been eyeing a trade opportunity for a few days, and now everything is perfectly aligned, so you enter the trade. Shortly after, the market dips, then rises slightly, only to dip again, hitting your stop loss. To make matters worse, it then reverses and skyrockets. This situation, undoubtedly frustrating, is one many traders have experienced. It's tough, truly. There are two ways you can respond to situations like these. The first option is to let emotions take over. You might feel anger, disappointment, or even a sense of injustice, followed by a strong urge to be made whole again at all costs. It's a typical human response to loss, but it frequently leads to detrimental outcomes for your trading performance and account. The second, more constructive option is to embrace such occurrences as a learning opportunity and a natural part of the process of trading. By "embrace," I don't suggest a superficial or merely intellectual acceptance, as I've hopefully made clear thus far; instead, I mean a profound, soul-deep surrender to the experience. These are two distinct experiences with vastly different implications. In surrender, the ego takes a back seat, and the desire for immediate gratification recedes. Instead, there is a wholehearted yielding to the process, letting things play out as they may without expecting anything in particular. Mindfulness serves as a catalyst for achieving such a state of graceful surrender to the process. By employing the S.T.A.Y. mnemonic, by becoming a student and practitioner of mindfulness, you create the right internal conditions for profitability, sustainability, and fulfillment.

As you engage in the process of cultivating your trading composure, here are three additional key points to consider:

1. Isolate Yourself from the Noise

A quick stroll around the various social media platforms will show you an onslaught of traders and analysts, pros and amateurs alike, sharing their trades and views on markets. The great abundance of trading styles, methods, and analyses shows that there is not a one-and-only way to trade. Consequently, everyone offers a unique perspective, and an attitude of openness to those diverse approaches and perspectives can only help inform your own understanding of things. However, it's crucial not to let these diverse views and opinions dictate your trading decisions, whether you are managing existing trades or planning new ones. Your own trading plan, methodology, and judgment should always take precedence, regardless of the expertise of others. If you wish to consider alternative viewpoints and potentially adjust your approach, it is better to do so when markets are closed and you have no active trades. When you allow external opinions to cause you to deviate from your established trading rules, you approach the market unstructured. That is another display of your intolerance of uncertainty. You are not confident in yourself and your strategy, and as a result, you blindly trust the apparent expertise of someone else. That person could indeed be an expert at what they do; however, it's important to remember that this doesn't automatically warrant abandoning your well-defined trading process in the heat of the moment to follow their lead. This impulsive shift is often a recipe for disaster.

On a personal note, this is one of the reasons why I refrain from using social media while actively trading, and that has had a significant impact on my mindset. In the past, when I used to engage with other traders' trades and analyses, I found myself becoming excessively anxious, filled with doubt, and less at ease. It fueled an obsession with immediate outcomes, pushing me to overmanage my positions. Learn to catch your own fish, utilizing your unique skills, methods, and tools rather than depending on others to provide sustenance. This is the only productive way forward. I've met a lot of traders over my years in this vibrant field, and I've yet to come across a consistently profitable trader who relies solely on social media stock picks and analyses. A self-sufficient approach to trading, relying on your own abilities and strategies, is the hallmark of successful traders. Your trading strategy and process are all that matters. That should be one of your guiding principles throughout your trading journey. Doing so allows you to position yourself for a more successful and sustainable experience.

2. Reconsider How You View Money

Naturally, money is the prime motivator for getting involved in the market, and there is nothing inherently amiss in that motivation. I've never met anyone who comes into the space thinking, "Oh, I'm just here to have fun." That said, money being the prime motivator makes trading difficult. Often, our performance suffers precisely because money is on our minds. This phenomenon isn't unique to the world of trading; it extends to various domains, including professional sports. Ask any pro athlete, and you will get the same answer: Obsessing about the end goal, whether the prize or the fame, creates pressure, which often derails performance.

Consequently, to perform better, it's crucial to put our money concerns and obsessions on the back burner and instead focus on performing well. As previously discussed, the S.T.A.Y. method should help facilitate this. However, it is also beneficial to occasionally contemplate the true nature of things as we often generate emotional attachment toward things that aren't what they seem. Take money—it is undoubtedly important in our lives. But if you take a moment to ponder its essence, you'll realize that, inherently, money holds no intrinsic value. It is essentially a piece of paper, metal, and nowadays just some lines of computer codes. Its nature is devoid of any objective worth, unlike essentials like food and water that sustain us. We only think money is worth something because society has seared in our mind a narrative about it. And if everybody believes that narrative, it works. Value emerges out of nothing.

To reiterate, I'm not denying the importance of money in society. Trivializing it would be insensitive, particularly when many people worldwide face the daily struggle of putting food on their tables due to financial constraints. However, it's essential to strike a balanced perspective. Striking this balance allows us to appreciate the significance of money while preventing it from dominating our thoughts and actions to the detriment of our overall well-being and bottom-line results. Setting time aside to examine the fundamental constituents of things can help us achieve that balanced perspective, thereby breaking some of the attachments one may have toward them. In the case of money, this shift in perspective can facilitate a more enlightened and composed approach to trading. Remember: if you need money, simply focus on trading well and the money will take care of itself. It will naturally follow as a consequence of your disciplined efforts. Conversely, fixating on money and allowing your emotions to take control will only delay its manifestation in your life.

3. Mind Your Use of Technology

As previously mentioned, the S.T.A.Y. process is designed to help you integrate mindfulness into your daily routine. However, if you're simultaneously killing your attention span and mindfulness capacity through indiscriminate technology use, you're doing yourself a disservice. I'm not suggesting that you completely abstain from using social media or even throw away your phone. Instead, I recommend establishing clear guidelines for your technology usage. When you find yourself endlessly scrolling through social media, what you're often seeking is a quick "feel-good" fix. It's a bad habit to reinforce because you're conditioning your mind toward short-term emotional gratification. You are caught in a loop of watching videos or looking at people's opinions and lives, and once you're down that rabbit hole, it isn't easy to get out. Recall the lesson on neuroplasticity we discussed earlier: What you frequently practice becomes the norm for your mind. You are actively molding the patterns and inclinations of your life. And trading success is hindered by such mindless pursuit of fleeting emotional rewards.

To become an exceptional trader, you must cultivate a different mindset and approach to your life. I'm not suggesting that you need to become a saint or a monk; instead, I'm saying that most traders fail not because they lack the right strategy but because they lack the right mindset. To join the ranks of profitable traders, you must do what these unsuccessful traders aren't doing. You must take care of your mind by first cultivating its innate capacity for perspective, presence, and wisdom. You also need to nourish it with the right content. Finally, you need to set reasonable limits on your technology usage. You could decide to check social media only once or twice a week. This is just an example; the appropriate limit is one that feels manageable for you. The goal isn't to eliminate all sources of information or completely disconnect from the world. The idea is not to be controlled by information or technology; it's to stop reinforcing bad habits and become more discerning. Your attention matters more than you might think—invest it in things and people that make your life better, not worse.

Perspective Through and Through

As I pen these lines, my friend is across the room, sitting on the couch, lost in her favorite TV show. Every so often, her eyelids flutter, her lips part, her countenance shifts, and the sound of her breath reaches my ears. She's wholly immersed in a state of pure experience while her thoughts seem momentarily at rest. In contrast, I'm entangled in my own ruminations.

The nature of mind captivates me deeply. Take thoughts, for instance. They're quite the conundrum. Their origins, their fleeting nature, their tangibility or lack thereof, our inability to halt their relentless march, our propensity to become ensnared by them—such enigmas hang on the periphery of my awareness every now and then. Ironically, it is the very act of thought that prompts me to contemplate its essence. Thought itself leads me to think about thought, trapping me in an endless, self-perpetuating loop. The mind is an enigmatic expanse where experiences arise and dissolve with an almost dreamlike quality. But so, too, is life. Or could it be that mind and life are one and the same? Amidst these musings, questions multiply while answers remain elusive.

Life is a paradox. One could even say that it's inherently absurd. It presents itself as a maze of contradictions, where light and darkness intertwine, where joy and sorrow dance hand in hand, where success and failure are but two sides of the same coin, where growth emerges from adversity, and where the pursuit of happiness often leads us through moments of uncertainty. Life is indeed a perplexing journey. It is a mystery unfolding moment by moment, an intricate tapestry of events and circumstances. Given that inherent mystery and uncertainty, the fundamental questions of existence often linger in the back of our heads unbeknownst to us: Why do we exist? Why are things as they are? What is the true meaning or purpose behind this shared experience we call life? What ultimate goal, if any, are we striving toward? Why does life seem fair for some and unfair for others; why are there injustices? Why is there suffering? If there is a God, why does he seem to be sleeping on the job? These questions, and others, are hard to contemplate because they go without tangible answers; hence, most people don't even engage them for fear of getting drawn into a vortex of pessimism, disillusionment, and overwhelm, where the beauty and potential of life are overshadowed by a focus on its more troubling aspects. Others choose to remain willfully blind in the face of such realities by set-tling for simplistic explanations in the form of age-old stories and narratives or new-age ones. This isn't a pejorative judgment; it is simply an observation.

Ultimately, life is what it is, and more importantly, it is what we make of it. Let me share a captivating story I heard years ago that illustrates this notion. In this tale, a dog wandered into a museum where every surface—the walls, ceiling, and floor—consisted of mirrors. The moment the dog stepped inside, it was immediately confronted by a seemingly endless array of dogs gazing back at it. Feeling cornered and threatened, the dog responded with growls and defensive barking. To its astonishment, each mirror reflected these aggressive actions, intensifying the hostility in the room. Trapped in this overwhelming feedback cycle, the dog grew increas-ingly frantic, snapping and barking incessantly. By morning, when the museum staff discovered the dog, it was curled up in a corner, trembling, exhausted, and battered. The poor dog had worn itself out by engaging in futile battles with its own reflections. Later that same day, another dog ventured into the same room but left moments later, its tail happily wagging. The moral of the story is clear: When the joyful dog entered the room, it likely encountered a multitude of happy dogs in the mirrors. Conversely, the angry dog was met with a multitude of growling faces, each reflection reinforcing the negativ-ity and hostility it harbored within. It is with life as it is with the mirror—how we experience life and what we perceive in the world around us often reflects the state of our own inner being. Life, in its essence, is a canvas upon which we paint our realities.

Life aside, the market, too, is akin to a mirror that reflects a trader's own beliefs, emotions, and biases. The angry dog, con-fronted by what he perceived as threats, responded with aggression and panic. Similarly, a trader operating from a place of fear or greed might perceive market movements as more hostile or promising than they truly are. These heightened emotions can cloud judg-ment, leading to reactionary decisions rather than informed choices. The happy dog, on the other hand, saw a room full of potential play-mates. In trading, this would be analogous to an individual who approaches the markets with trading composure. Such a trader is likelier to spot genuine opportunities and act on them in a balanced manner. Such a trader is likelier to go through losses with a positive attitude. This story is a reminder for all traders. The markets will always reflect our deepest-held beliefs and feelings about trading, money, and a plethora of other things. By approaching trading with a balanced mindset and a positive perspective, we can ensure that our "reflections" are aligned with the market's requirements for success.

Having expressed that, I'm fully aware that putting this into practice is far from simple. Our perceptions are often deeply ingrained through years of conditioning, becoming the default mode of how we see the world. When faced with an adverse market move, for instance, there's the typical pattern that unfolds:

1. The move occurs.
2. The event is instantly perceived and interpreted based on past experiences.
3. Emotions arise in response to the meaning assigned to it.

This sequence unfolds in mere moments. But what if you consciously became aware of the inner narrative playing in your mind, such as how this situation is negative, how discouraged or cheated you feel, or how much of a loser you are for not having anticipated the move? What if you consciously and deliberately challenged that immediate narrative? For example, if you catch the narrative and notice yourself getting worked up because of it, reframe the situation. Instead of labeling it as entirely negative, consider it as a valuable learning experience. Replace feelings of discouragement with determination to improve. Tell yourself that diamonds are formed from coal under extreme pressure. In essence, view the challenging experience as essential for your growth as a trader and affirm your commitment to face it with resilience and a positive outlook. This will empower and motivate you rather than cause distress.

One crucial point to underscore: This reframing isn't necessarily done with the purpose of believing the narrative; rather, the purpose is to bring up any unconscious material that would like to argue with that new narrative. If the event is particularly painful emotionally, chances are you'll sense a reflexive surge of energy, a sort of resistance, in response to the new narrative you're trying to instill. This energy typically gains momentum when it arises unseen; at some point, it defaults you back to your old perceptions and interpretations. However, in this deliberate process of altering your perception by affirming a different interpretation of the event, you are consciously summoning and acknowledging it, accepting it fully, and then relaxing into it. When you observe the energy, refrain from labeling it as "good" or "bad." There's no need for mental rationalization or analysis; simply be present with it, accepting it with kindness until it naturally subsides—it always does. If you can practice this after each adverse event in the market, those events will have a harder time triggering you. However, if you don't notice this energy and how it fuels a stream of inner stories, justifications, and judgments, along with accompanying emotions, or worse, if you notice it and reject it, adverse events will have an easier time triggering you, much like the first dog was triggered by countless reflections of himself.

Approaching our internal world from a phenomenological perspective requires us to become both participants and observers of our own mental processes deliberately and continuously. This brings us back to a point I've emphasized earlier: It is crucial to take proactive control of the process of rewiring your mindset for success in trading. Don't leave it up to the vagaries of chance. Every moment presents an opportunity to practice and reinforce the qualities and thought patterns you wish to instill in your mind. Whether it's strategically placed Post-It notes on your trading desk, practicing composure while waiting in traffic, or being present with your children or partner, understand that every moment, every day, the actions you take—every single one of them!—is a vote for the kind of person and trader you aspire to become. Don't underestimate the significance of these seemingly small details—they are anything but small. How you do one thing is how you do everything; hence, tread carefully and sculpt your mind and reality in a way that your future self will be proud of.

Chapter 4
The Accountability Factor

The Institutional Trader's Edge

In the previous chapter, we discussed the significance of mindfulness as a tool to develop one's trading composure. I understand that nurturing a mindfulness practice isn't easy and that routines like S.T.A.Y. may seem dull, but that's precisely what trading requires—a thoughtful, purposeful, and methodical approach to each day. Trading is simple in principle; it's just about getting one to do the little things that cumulatively lead to substantial achievements. However, therein lies the challenge—doing the little things isn't exactly what one would call easy. Unfortunately, we frequently become ensnared in the narratives of our minds. Nonetheless, consider this: What other option do you have? If your aim is to be fully engaged in your life and generate improved outcomes, whether in trading or any other aspect, you must dive in and do those little things. At this very moment and in every moment, we possess the potential to evolve into enhanced versions of ourselves. Where there's a will, there's a way. The key lies in being clear about why consistency in trading is important to you and getting viscerally connected to that goal.

Another one of these "little things" crucial to the project of profitable trading is the idea of personal accountability. Now, what makes accountability so important that I present it as the third and final pillar to trading success? Well, to put it simply, on the retail end, trading is characterized by autonomy; your actions account for roughly 80% of your success, with the remaining 20% being shaped by market dynamics and external variables. From my standpoint, this autonomy was, in fact, a significant factor that drew me to the trading world, as it meant that I would have the freedom to shape my own outcomes. Additionally, being the introvert I am, the prospect of working independently, without needing to navigate team and leadership dynamics, was particularly appealing. However, being autonomous and independent also meant that I had to own up to the results I was getting; I had to stay accountable to myself.

Personal accountability in trading encompasses two critical elements: Firstly, there is pre-trade accountability, which is about establishing a clear vision of your ultimate objective as a trader—namely, to attain consistency. This involves continuously reminding yourself of this overarching goal and ensuring that each decision you make in the heat of the moment is in harmony with this long-term aspiration. This proactive alignment requires consciously asking yourself whether the impending trading decision will contribute to or detract from your desired state of consistent trading. For instance, consider a scenario where you're in the market, and emotions start to surge as you witness a trade you missed taking off. You're torn between the urge to enter the trade hastily, convinced it will continue to climb higher, and the cautious voice inside reminding you that it might be too late and entering now could be a mistake. Pre-decision accountability comes into play when you pause to evaluate this opportunity against your goal of achieving consistency. You might ask yourself, "Does entering this trade align with my established trading plan and risk management rules, or am I being swayed by the potential for quick gains?" This moment of reflection is crucial. It's where you decide to either proceed with the trade because it meets your criteria for consistency or you choose to pass on it because it represents a departure from your disciplined trading approach. This is the essence of pre-decision accountability—you are making deliberate, goal-aligned choices before acting, and this preemptive scrutiny acts as a compass, guiding your actions toward your goal even before you commit to a decision.

Secondly, personal accountability extends into the realm of post-trade analysis. After a trading decision has been executed, it is crucial to thoroughly review the outcomes in relation to the predefined rules and benchmarks you have set for your trading. This retrospective examination involves more than just tallying wins and losses; it is a reflective process where you dissect the intricacies of each trade to unearth the underlying factors contributing to its success or failure. For instance, when a trade goes as planned, a trader practicing accountability doesn't just celebrate the win but also analyzes why the decision was successful. Was it due to a well-timed entry based on sound analysis and rules adherence, or was the trade successful merely because of luck? Conversely, a loss isn't just a loss. It's an opportunity to reflect on what might have gone wrong. Did you stray from your trading plan, or was it a function of the normal distribution of wins and losses? This post-decision accountability necessitates setting up a system for tracking and reviewing the insights you are gathering, such as a trading journal. Over time, this journal becomes invaluable, enabling you to document your thought processes, market conditions, and emotional state for each trade. It builds into a comprehensive record that can reveal patterns in your trading behavior, areas for improvement, and strategies that yield the best results.

So, as you can see, accountability is a cycle of continuous learning and adaptation, where each trade—regardless of its immediate financial outcome—serves as a building block in your journey toward becoming a more disciplined and effective trader. Together, these two aspects of personal accountability form a holistic approach to trading that prioritizes strategic alignment with long-term goals and fosters a culture of rigorous self-assessment and continuous improvement. This dual focus ensures that you remain steadfast on your path to trading consistency, equipped with the insights and discipline to refine your strategies and decision-making processes continuously. It's important to note that personal accountability presents a significant challenge, as evidenced by the widespread struggle to adhere to diets, maintain a regular gym routine, or consistently practice meditation. These everyday commitments already test our self-discipline and resolve. Now, consider the amplified complexity of maintaining this level of accountability in the high-pressure trading arena, where the stakes are high as they include not just personal goals but also financial risks. The task becomes exponentially more daunting. Hence, there's a third dimension to accountability, crucial for success in trading, that most retail traders commonly overlook: External accountability.

External accountability involves becoming part of a framework or partnership where someone else, such as a mentor, coach, or peer group, observes and assesses your trading actions and decisions. This outside perspective can provide objective feedback, helping to highlight areas for improvement that might not be evident from a solo viewpoint. Consider the importance billionaire trader Paul Tudor Jones places on such external accountability. In his relentless pursuit of disciplined trading, he turned to Tony Robbins, the renowned life coach. Tudor Jones's commitment to being accountable to Robbins meant that he was more diligent in adhering to his trading strategies and plans, fully aware that his actions would undergo scrutiny and discussion. This bolstered his dedication to trading objectives and improved his overall trading performance. Robbins's guidance was a pillar for Tudor Jones, supporting him through prosperous periods and challenging times, leading to a more methodical and concentrated trading approach and experience. The two men have maintained this relationship since 1993, further underscoring Paul Tudor Jones's significant emphasis on cultivating the right psychology. This account illustrates a key point: Despite our best intentions, our commitment can falter under the weight of changing moods and temporary desires. Willpower, while potent, can be fickle, easily eroded by the day-to-day trials we face. Solely depending on it is risky. External accountability acts as a crucial support system, guiding us back on track when we stray. It amplifies our potential, serving as a co-pilot on our journey, ensuring we stay the course. Making a commitment to someone else, whether a mentor, coach, or peer group, does more than just articulate our goals; it cements our commitment to them, fostering a reciprocal dynamic where growth and progress flourish.

Paul Tudor Jones aside, institutional traders, as a whole, consistently outperform retail traders. What is interesting to note is that the folks who go on to become institutional traders are often recruited fresh from college or university. Their selection is primarily based on academic achievements; most lack substantial real-world trading experience. Despite this lack of experience, their trading performances far exceed average retail traders. Therefore, the question arises: what gives institutional traders this edge? What explains their performance gap with retail traders? It's crucial to grasp that the edge held by institutional traders isn't an informational one but financial and structural ones. Financially, the vast resources at their disposal allow for a better mitigation of risk through a variety of risk strategies, such as hedging and diversification. Structurally, the environment in which they operate is designed to enforce discipline and adherence to strategy. Institutional traders work under the watchful eyes of accountability managers or risk officers who monitor their every move, ensuring strict compliance with risk allotments and trading protocols. This framework promotes a disciplined and process-oriented approach to trading. In contrast, retail traders navigate the market solo, acting as their own supervisors. This autonomy is indeed liberating and, in the long term, can be immensely rewarding for those who achieve proficiency. However, in the early stages of a trading career, or even when one is simply struggling to maintain behavioral consistency, the absence of external accountability can be a significant hurdle. Without a professional mentor or a coach to provide objective feedback, guidance, and sometimes the necessary "tough love," staying on the path to consistency can be challenging, to put it mildly.

The significance of external accountability is backed by robust scientific evidence and research. For example, research conducted by the American Society of Training and Development (ASTD) reveals that people have a 65% chance of achieving their goals when they commit to someone else. And this likelihood increases to 95% when they commit to a professional, like a seasoned coach or a dedicated accountability manager (Hanke 2018). This underlines the reason why eminent figures like Paul Tudor Jones, as well as trading firms in general, place a high value on external accountability— it's a proven strategy for consistency and success! Retail traders neglecting external accountability, assuming that they can manage on their own, are ultimately doing themselves a disservice. Echoing the sentiments expressed in the previous chapter on mindfulness, one must ask: if your competitors are employing specific techniques and practices to increase their competitive edge, wouldn't it be wise to explore what they're doing and consider adopting those strategies yourself? Ponder this . . .

The DIY Method: Good or Bad?

What I'm about to say might come across as a shameless plug for my coaching program. However, I urge you to hear me before jumping to that conclusion. Trading is quite simple in principle, and it's easy to fall into the trap of thinking that success is easily attainable through a do-it-yourself approach. The reality, of course, is far more complex. Imagine being thrown into an arena with some of the world's most intelligent, well-equipped, well-researched, and well-funded people, all of whom are, in some ways, your direct competitors. Your capital is at stake, and, in a broader sense, so is your livelihood. This is the essence of trading. To survive and prosper in this competitive environment, one must strive to become part of the exclusive circle of traders who achieve consistent success. This path requires mastering both the market's technical intricacies and the mental hurdles that accompany them, and traveling this journey solo only amplifies the challenge.

As traders, it can be hard for us to accept help. We're often DIY (do-it-yourself) enthusiasts, which can hinder our willingness to seek the help we need. In fields like athletics, business, performance arts, or even spirituality, seeking guidance and support from a coach or mentor is a well-accepted practice. People recognize the value of expert advice to navigate the complexities of their chosen paths. However, when it comes to trading, many seem to hold a contrary perspective. The apparent simplicity of trading—where the market either rises or falls—leads many to underestimate its challenges. They often think, "I can do this on my own; I don't need a mentor or coach." While the DIY approach may appear cost-effective and straightforward, it often turns out to be the most costly route. Mistakes quickly add up, leading to not just expensive financial losses but also emotional trauma. This trauma traps traders in a cycle where fear from past mistakes dictates their trading decisions. This is a common scenario for many self-taught traders who, in an attempt to save on the cost of a good coach or mentor, end up shooting down their chances of success.

A mentor or coach can help steer you clear of common pitfalls, potentially saving you significant money in the long run. This is because mastering skills like embracing uncertainty and managing emotions is crucial for profitable trading, yet these don't come easily to many. Speaking from personal experience, I know the struggle all too well. Despite achieving market consistency on my own, without any formal coach or mentor, it was a grueling five-year journey marked by losses and frustration over my inability to shift away from unprofitable habits. While I eventually reached my goals using the DIY method, looking back, I would have greatly benefited from the guidance of a seasoned coach or mentor to expedite my progress. Such support could have spared me considerable time, effort, financial loss, and spirit-breaking challenges. It would have simplified my path significantly.

The DIY approach often means embarking on the trading journey and learning along the way. This is a commendable thing to do; however, you must expect a lot of detours and roadblocks. The key differentiator between successful traders and those who struggle often lies in the questions they pose. The top traders don't just ask how to solve a problem or achieve a goal; they ask, "Who can help me reach my destination?" This shift in perspective is transformative, as seeking the right guidance is akin to gaining a navigator who knows both the obstacles and the efficient shortcuts. This guidance can provide a clear, tested roadmap to achieving your trading objectives. To be clear, the DIY route, too, can eventually lead you to your goals, but it comes with significant drawbacks. This approach often extends the journey, introduces greater uncertainty, and demands tolerance for delays and errors. Therefore, if you're aiming for substantial and swift advancements in your trading, consider this advice: invest in a coach—ideally, a seasoned one who understands your journey and has already helped others like you achieve their trading goals. The value such a coach can bring is immeasurable. They'll offer more than just structure, guidance, and accountability; they also provide a sense of partnership and camaraderie, reminding you that you're not navigating this path alone. This personal touch creates a supportive environment that no digital tool can match, enhancing your trading journey with both expertise and emotional support.

Trading in the retail sphere can be an isolating journey. In this era dominated by technology, the significance of human connection cannot be overstated. Despite the advancements and conveniences brought about by digital tools, the value of interpersonal interactions, especially in high-stakes environments like trading, remains irreplaceable. The lack of such a support system often traps traders in a cycle of self-sabotage, leading to a continuous emotional and performance rollercoaster. Pivoting to my work with traders, it is rooted in a comprehensive grasp of what works and doesn't. Within my coaching framework, we nurture a culture centered around the embrace of uncertainty, emotional stability, and accountability. My students benefit from a blend of structure and interpersonal interaction, enabling them to harness the proven advantages of ongoing composure, clear goals, precise measurements, and accountability, all while retaining full autonomy over their direction. Consider it akin to having a proficient guide and helpful teammates who are there to help you bridge the gap between you now and your future best self. This immersive experience around consistency ensures that the rational you and the monkey-brain you collaborate effectively to fulfill your trading aspirations.

To reiterate, you can reach your trading goals without a formal coach or mentor, just like I did. The chief question is time—how much time do you want it to take? Everyone enters the trading world with unique backgrounds and predispositions. Your journey to success could be swift or stretch over years. My point is that by collaborating with a seasoned coach or mentor, your path to success gets shorter and more predictable. Choosing to work with someone is not an admission of weakness or inferiority; instead, it's a strategic move, an acknowledgment that the right support can move you closer to your goals. Recognizing the need for assistance and acting on it is a sign of strength, as it demonstrates a commitment to self-improvement and the wisdom to leverage available resources for personal and professional growth.

It is often said that becoming a consistently profitable trader can take years. This is an accurate statement, generally speaking; however, this timeline can be significantly shortened to just a few months by surrounding yourself with the right people. For instance, in my coaching program, we have a remarkably high success rate, over 95%, in transforming struggling traders into consistent performers. This achievement stems from my belief in compatibility. I have no interest in enrolling students who are unlikely to succeed in our program. To me, it's not just about numbers; it's about fit. I only work with a small group and don't simply take on new students; instead, I form partnerships with individuals committed to their own success. While I can't promise specific financial gains due to market uncertainties, I do guarantee to foster behavioral consistency among those I mentor if they show up in the program. This behavioral consistency is key to achieving steady trading results without the emotional rollercoaster. But, again, for the magic to happen, the student needs to be ready; hence, I don't enroll new students unless I'm 100% sure that is the case. Your journey with me will be as successful as your commitment to it.

Now, my program aside, there are other good trading coaches and mentors out there. People tend to think that all trading educators are simply failed traders trying to capitalize on newbies. This is sloppy thinking. Yes, some trading educators are running scams;

however, there are many reputable and knowledgeable ones who genuinely like to help others improve their trading skills and achieve their financial goals. Many wish to share their knowledge and are invested in their students' success. The key is for you to exercise caution and discernment. Avoid getting swayed by superficial displays like luxury cars, private jets, or manipulated profit screenshots, which are likely not as they seem. Focus on the real value and steer clear of traders who try hard to impress you with a know-it-all demeanor and bold promises with questionable evidence. Even though you might undoubtedly learn a thing or two from them, quite often, such individuals are themselves trapped in a prediction mindset; hence, they are unlikely to provide the insights that truly matter in trading, let alone the expert support needed to activate the flywheel effect of progress.

Staying Consistent with A.C.T.

Nothing can level you up faster than ongoing feedback from a professional tracking your every move in the market. Sometimes, their feedback might be harsh, but its purpose isn't to break you; it's to help you grow. In my coaching practice, before welcoming anyone into my select circle of consistent traders, I candidly inquire: "I will be providing you with some tough love at times if I see that you're not following through with what you said you were going to do. Are you OK with this? Are you prepared for constructive criticism when your actions don't align with your commitments?" Typically, the response from prospective students eager to join my coaching program is affirmative—their heart is, indeed, in the right place. However, you'd be surprised to see how often students, initially so eager and affirmative, struggle when faced with the reality of constructive criticism.

In my years of working with traders, I've honed my ability to detect subtle signs that indicate whether or not a potential student is a good fit for my program. If, during an initial consultation, I detect signs that we are not the right match to work together, I don't take their payment, I don't enroll them. I still ensure they get value from the consultation; however, it marks the point where our journey concludes. My commitment is to work only with individuals I am confident I can assist—those who are not only ready to take initiative in their own growth but also display a strong desire to learn and a willingness to be coached. Without that, even personalized guidance from renowned motivator Tony Robbins will fall on barren ground. My practice is rooted in the belief that the real transformation begins when the individual's paradigm shifts toward growth and resilience; my role as a coach is to catalyze and nurture this transformation.

Now, whether you work with someone or not, for accountability to be effective, it needs to be structured around key principles that ensure consistent progress and personal growth. I've developed a mnemonic, A.C.T., to encapsulate these principles, making them easier to remember and apply.

A.C.T. stands for:

- A: Acknowledge Progress and Setbacks
- C: Commitment to the Journey
- T: Take Full Ownership

Let's explore each one individually:

A: *Acknowledge Progress and Setbacks*

Picture this: You're embarking on a hiking adventure with the goal of reaching the summit of a majestic mountain. Along the way, you encounter breathtaking vistas, and as you ascend, you celebrate each milestone achieved—whether it's reaching a scenic overlook or conquering a particularly steep incline. These moments of progress fuel your determination and bolster your spirits. They serve as reminders of your resilience and the rewards that come from perseverance. However, the path to the summit isn't without its challenges. There are times when you encounter unexpected setbacks—a sudden downpour, a twisted ankle, or a wrong turn that leads you off course. In those moments, it's easy to feel disheartened or frustrated. Yet, it's precisely during these times of adversity that growth occurs. Reflecting on your setbacks, you glean valuable insights and lessons. Perhaps you realize the importance of packing a rain jacket or investing in better hiking boots. Maybe you learn to listen more closely to your intuition or to adapt to changing circumstances with grace and flexibility. The key lies in maintaining a balanced perspective—a perspective that celebrates victories, however small, while also constructively addressing mistakes. It's about embracing the duality of progress and setbacks, recognizing that both are essential components of the journey.

Now, trading is just like that. Victories come in the form of successful trades, profitable strategies, or moments of clarity amidst market uncertainty. These victories fuel our confidence, motivate us to continue, and validate our efforts. Yet, alongside these triumphs, there are inevitable setbacks—losses, mistakes, and periods of increased uncertainty. It's essential to maintain the same spirit we exhibit in hiking—celebrating successes while acknowledging setbacks. Pain, in the form of losses or unexpected turns in the market, is part of the trading process. Just as a hiker prepares for adverse weather conditions or challenging terrain, a trader must be prepared for the chaotic nature of the market. They must anticipate losses and practice proper risk management; they must remain stable in their resolve, flexible in their expectations, and consistent with their process in the face of changing circumstances. Embracing this mindset allows traders to navigate the highs and lows of the market with composure. It encourages them to approach trading with a sense of curiosity, humility, and a willingness to learn from both successes and failures.

Ultimately, it's the ability to maintain perspective, acknowledge progress and setbacks, and embrace the challenges inherent in the trading journey that distinguishes successful traders. As with any journey, the path to trading mastery requires patience, perseverance, and an unwavering commitment to growth. So, as you embark on your trading journey, remember: Pain is part of the process. Expect it, accept it! In doing that, you cultivate a growth mindset—a mindset that thrives on continuous learning and development. That said, don't forget to celebrate your victories also; all in all, embrace the adventure ahead.

C: Commitment to the Journey

I have a deep appreciation for stories that carry profound messages, particularly those rooted in the Zen tradition. These tales often appear enigmatic and perplexing at first glance, yet upon closer examination, they reveal layers of profound wisdom and insight.

Allow me to share one that I love:

Once upon a time, a young boy playing along the shoreline noticed an elderly man in the distance. The man was sitting in a squat position with his gaze fixed downward. Intrigued, the boy approached and observed the man meticulously drawing a flawless circle in the sand.

"Hey, old man! How did you manage to draw such a perfect circle?" the boy inquired with genuine curiosity.

Without looking up, the man responded calmly, "I cannot say, my child. I simply attempted, failed, and persisted . . . Here, why don't you give it a try?"

With that, the man handed the boy the drawing implement and quietly walked away. Puzzled yet determined, the boy began his own attempts at drawing circles in the sand. Initially, his circles were uneven, misshapen, and far from perfect. However, undeterred, he persisted in his efforts, striving for improvement with each attempt.

As time passed, the boy's circles gradually improved, becoming smoother and more symmetrical. One radiant morning, after relentless practice, he finally succeeded in crafting a flawless circle in the sand. It was then that he heard a faint voice behind him.

"Excuse me, old man . . . How did you manage to draw such a perfect circle?"

This poignant story underscores the profound lesson of perseverance, practice, and the journey toward mastery. The "circle" (called Enso, or Ensō) is a sacred symbol in Zen. Traditionally drawn with a single brushstroke, the Enso embodies the meditative practice of letting go of the mind and allowing the body to create—a process devoid of alterations or corrections. The story reminds us that greatness is not achieved overnight but through dedication, resilience, and unwavering determination—a testament to the adage that practice makes perfect.

As traders, we often perceive success as a distant destination—a shimmering beacon on the horizon that seems perpetually out of reach. This perspective can be discouraging, leading to impatience and frustration when immediate results fail to materialize. Compounding this issue is the societal emphasis on instant gratification, fostering a culture of impatience and short attention spans. In today's dopamine-driven world, individuals are conditioned to seek rapid rewards, abandoning pursuits at the slightest hint of adversity. However, what if we shifted our focus away from fleeting gratification and instead directed our attention toward the journey leading to our desired goals? Like any skill, trading mastery demands relentless dedication, engagement, and deliberate practice, often with no immediate payoff—nothing but losses to show for one's efforts. However, examining the stories of successful traders reveals a common thread: they understand that the journey to trading mastery is not a sprint but a marathon—a continuous process of discovery, learning, and adjustment. Regardless of one's style or time frame, trading is inherently a statistical probability game; hence, by default, that makes it a long game. The nature of statistics makes it so that you can't put too much significance on one data point. Attaching your self-worth, dreams, hopes, and aspirations to one trade, or even a few of them, is counterproductive, to say the least. Any statistically based pursuits demand that you stay emotionally and personally detached from the process, assessing your results over longer periods. Struggling traders don't operate like that. They're typically taught trading from marketers, not real traders, who promote trading as a pathway to quick wealth. However, as this book has demonstrated thus far, such notions are far from accurate. While there exists the potential for rapid life-changing gains, this path is not the norm.

Fundamentally, trading is a long game; it's a game of probabilities centered around self-mastery, which necessitates time and a commitment to the journey. Just as the young boy learned to draw a perfect circle through dedication and unwavering determination, aspiring traders must approach their craft with a similar mindset.

By embracing the journey, with its ups and downs, and focusing on continuous improvement, traders can navigate the challenges of the market with resilience and grit.

T: Take Full Ownership

Accountability goes beyond merely adhering to rules or guidelines; it involves being honest and forthcoming about every aspect of one's trading journey. This transparency begins with oneself, as traders must first be candid with their own motivations, intentions, and actions; traders distinguish themselves when they take full responsibility for the outcomes they get. They set themselves apart when they abandon the victim mentality.

For many, everything is someone or something else's fault. Here is how to immediately spot losing traders: Read through any trading forum or online discussion, and see who is talking about slippage, stop hunting, and thieving brokers all in the same sentence. Odds are, they are the ones. Those are the people who are constantly looking for external factors to blame for their lack of success in the markets. They often point fingers at trade tipsters, market manipulation, unfair practices, or even conspiracy theories rather than examining their own trading strategies and decision-making processes. This mindset is a clear indicator of a losing trader because it reveals an unwillingness to take personal responsibility for their actions and outcomes. These individuals are typically more invested in justifying their failures than in learning from their mistakes. They prefer to believe that the fault rests on the external rather than acknowledging that trading involves inherent risks and uncertainties that every trader must learn to navigate.

Traders progress once they take full responsibility for their trading decisions and put a stop to the victim complex and cycle of blame. From my end, when I understood that I alone was responsible for my trading decisions and what happened to me in the market, not brokers, Jim Cramer, tipsters, or even the cat, real progress began. Taking full ownership of your results is undoubtedly scary. Nobody likes to be wrong or blamed; those things are uncomfortable. However, it is empowering to realize that you are in the driver's seat; you choose your actions and responses. You have control over your thoughts and what you emit into the world, even though external events might not always be in your control.

To be clear, it isn't helpful to dwell on your mistakes or short-comings. That would be operating from a loser's mindset—again. Instead, I'm suggesting you acknowledge your central role in the results you are getting and vow to make better decisions. Take responsibility and allow yourself to grow to a new level of consciousness where you are able to make different choices, leading to different outcomes. This honesty paves the way for an empowering mindset and tremendous personal growth. Without ownership of your actions, you remain trapped; avoidance and denial prevent you from confronting challenges head-on, leaving you at the mercy of external forces and stuck in unproductive patterns, especially in the chaotic world of trading.

It is crucial to grasp that you, and only you, are in charge of your life, your decisions, and the results you achieve. I can't emphasize this enough! Imagine someone blaming a gym owner for their lack of fitness progress instead of acknowledging their responsibility in their own fitness journey. I'm aware that some people, indeed, do this; however, what I'm saying is that this attitude doesn't work! This mindset of shifting blame is not just unfair; it hinders your ability to learn and grow.

Owning your failures and successes alike—the good, the bad, and the ugly—creates a different inner experience and positions you as the architect of your destiny. "What can I learn from this?" and "How can I improve?" This is a foundational principle you must embrace if you plan to be happy and successful.

* * *

Trading isn't a scam; it's a probability game centered around self-mastery. You can learn to play that game well, but it takes time and commitment. The journey toward trading proficiency involves more than just understanding market trends and financial instruments; it demands a deep dive into one's own psychological makeup.

Traders must cultivate patience, emotional resilience, and an analytical mindset to make informed decisions amidst the markets' chaotic dances. This introspective process is crucial for developing the trading composure required to withstand the inevitable ups and downs of trading. Moreover, a commitment to lifelong learning is indispensable in the ever-evolving landscape of trading. Markets are dynamic and influenced by myriad factors; hence, staying informed and adaptable is paramount. In that regard, accountability is crucial.

Accountability in trading, or any endeavor, is the cornerstone of success and personal growth. It's about taking ownership of your actions, decisions, and their outcomes. In the context of trading, this means being responsible for your trading plan, risk management strategies, and emotional responses to market fluctuations. Accountability involves a commitment to evaluating your performance honestly, learning from both successes and failures, and continuously seeking ways to improve.

That said, accountability also extends beyond self-assessment; it involves creating a transparent system where your decisions and actions can be reviewed and critiqued, either by a mentor or coach or through a personal trading journal. This helps reinforce discipline, provides new perspectives on your trading approach, and keeps complacency at bay. In that accountability work, the A.C.T mnemonic can serve as a guiding principle. This structured approach ensures that traders are constantly learning, adapting, and growing in their craft, positioning them for long-term success in the markets.

Chapter 5
Parting Thoughts

Takeaways

Let me condense the essential insights from this book into three quotes, accompanied by a few reflections.

The first one comes from renowned American investor, the "Oracle of Omaha," Warren Buffett:

"The fact that people will be full of greed, fear, or folly is predictable. The sequence is not predictable."

Financial markets are fundamentally driven by human emotions and behavior. These emotional responses stem from a range of factors, including psychological biases, social influences, and economic circumstances. They can impact not only single individuals but also groups and whole communities, giving rise to discernible behavioral patterns that, to some extent, can be anticipated. This predictability of human behavior is what makes general trends in markets broadly predictable, particularly over the long term, as these behavior patterns are readily observable on any market chart. However, since the specific order in which fear, greed, or folly appear among market participants is indeterminable due to the unique blend of experiences, viewpoints, and situations that shape each person's emotional responses, timing exact market turning points and predicting specific trade outcomes remain arduous.

Uncertainty is a fundamental aspect of both the market and trading dynamics. Different people have different opinions about when to buy or sell, what constitutes high or low prices, and myriad other factors. Hence, sometimes positive developments are met with selling pressure, and negative ones are met with buying pressure. Additionally, emotions can trigger or amplify these buying and selling pressures in reasonless ways. We see that time and time again. Consequently, you'll often hear trading pundits proclaim that short-term trade outcomes are randomly distributed. From my standpoint, I'm not making the argument that short-term trade outcomes are incontestably random. We can get into long philosophical debates about why they are and are not. What I'm saying instead is that it is useful to consider short-term outcomes as random. Through my extensive experience as a trader and having worked with a diverse array of traders globally in my trading psychology coaching practice, I've witnessed the substantial benefits of perceiving short-term trading outcomes as random occurrences. Here are three notable ones:

1. **Assuming randomness enhances risk awareness:** Many traders become emotionally invested in their trades, convinced by their analysis that profitability is assured. However, when these trades result in losses, the feeling of dismay, as if deceived or wronged, sets in. Adopting the perspective of randomness serves as a preemptive alert to possible losses or unforeseen outcomes, thus creating a mindset that is ready for anything.
2. **Assuming randomness simplifies decision-making:** Viewing trade outcomes as random encourages a focus on probabilities, akin to the simplicity of a coin toss where outcomes vary between winning and losing. A focus on probabilities forces us to understand what gives us a statistical edge, thereby enabling us to make more enlightened choices, while preventing undue fixation on specific trade outcomes.

3. **Assuming randomness helps us cultivate comfort with uncertainty:** When uncertainty is frequently brought to mind, it encourages emotional detachment from the outcome, instead directing our focus toward more significant, long-term elements such as strategy, behavioral consistency, and statistical rigor. Remarkably, this alleviates much of the stress associated with trading while allowing the mathematical logic of one's strategy to play out.

Once more, financial markets are a blend of predictable and unpredictable elements. While it's possible to discern trends and patterns, timing exact turning points is a challenging task, to put it mildly. Although the distribution of trade outcomes may display statistical regularities, foreseeing specific outcomes in advance is a formidable task given the multitude of moving elements directly impacting them, consequently echoing Warren Buffett's observation that *"the sequence of greed, fear, or folly is not predictable."*

Success in trading hinges on an acknowledgment of and comfort with this inherent uncertainty. This necessitates becoming a student of uncertainty, seeing it as a teacher and ally rather than a foe. In the first pillar of the book, we explored practical strategies for achieving this mindset shift. Through the F.A.C.E. mnemonic, I invited you to forge a harmonious relationship with uncertainty, laying the foundation for a more informed and resilient trading journey. Transitioning to the second pillar, allow me to share another quote, this one hailing from Shinzen Young, a distinguished author and meditation master in the Vipassana tradition:

"As long as something wants to arise, let it. As long as something wants to last, let it. As soon as something wants to pass, let it."

The next crucial phase in fostering a mindset that is geared for success in the chaotic realm of financial markets involves nurturing trading composure. In this phase, a more profound level of self-reflection and inner work is entirely necessary. In meditation circles, the term "monkey mind" describes an undisciplined and unaware state of mind. This concept metaphorically compares the human mind to a monkey: restless, erratic, and constantly shifting from one thought or urge to another. Such a mind is characterized by a lack of discipline and self-awareness, leading to a tendency to latch onto every fleeting feeling or impression, to easily get swayed by immediate gratifications, which usually undermine the pursuit of long-term goals and lasting satisfaction. This state of mind is particularly detrimental in situations that require strategic thinking and objectivity, such as trading. Being in the grip of the monkey mind makes one vulnerable to a host of pitfalls: cognitive biases and impulsive reactions, for example. Those are factors that can greatly overshadow a statistically sound trading strategy or system, leading to suboptimal trading decisions influenced more by fleeting emotions than reasoned analysis.

The root cause of the monkey mind can be traced back to an untrained and easily distracted attention span. This sets the stage for specific thought patterns to flourish, exerting influence over one's perception of the world and driving unwise reactions. However, as one begins the journey of training their focus and cultivating mindfulness, a transformative process unfolds. One gets better at interrupting the self-reinforcing cycle of the monkey mind. As the mind gradually becomes more stable and discerning, one's ability to respond to life's challenges and stimuli in a more deliberate and measured manner improves; one becomes less reactive and more proactive in one's choices and actions. The noise of the monkey mind diminishes, making space for inner calm and insight to emerge.

What makes meditation and mindfulness truly remarkable is that they are not confined to any particular belief system, nor do you need to align with any specific ideology to embrace these practices. For instance, you don't have to be a Buddhist or have any fondness for the Buddha; at its core, mindfulness is just pure awareness. When we cultivate mindfulness, our senses awaken to the world around us. Scents become vivid, textures rich to the touch, sounds crystal clear, and our vision sharpens. We immerse ourselves fully in the unfolding of each moment, observing the subtle shifts and transformations in our experiences. Mindfulness also extends to the realm of our thoughts. We learn to listen attentively to the inner dialogue without becoming entangled in its web. Likewise, we become attuned to the sensations arising in our bodies, neither clinging to the pleasant nor recoiling from the unpleasant. In this state of mindfulness, life flows seamlessly, and it offers a profound state of clarity and presence. Meditation provides us with a structured approach to cultivate and deepen this experience of pure awareness intentionally. It serves as a dedicated space and time to hone our mindfulness skills and refine our ability to stay present.

Establishing a meditation habit can be quite challenging. In fact, maintaining any habit presents its own set of difficulties. However, what makes meditation particularly demanding in today's technological era is the pervasive nature of distractions. Our attention is constantly pulled in multiple directions, making the practice of mindfulness even more arduous. The relentless digital onslaught, characterized by the incessant stream of notifications, emails, social media updates, and bite-sized content, conditions us to operate in short bursts of attention rather than fostering prolonged focus. This reinforces a craving for instant gratification and constant stimulation, which further fuels this perpetual state of distraction. The outcome is a scattered mind that readily succumbs to every passing whim, struggling to sustain concentration on a single task, vision, or objective for extended periods. Sadly, this condition runs counter to the sustained focus and discipline that meditation necessitates, let alone the demands of trading. Therefore, how can we effectively address this dilemma where we find ourselves lacking the mental fortitude to meditate yet recognizing the necessity of meditation to tame our monkey mind? Start by asking yourself a straightforward question: If you find it challenging to commit just 20 minutes a day to sit in silence, observing your breath and inner world, despite knowing the benefits of this practice, what makes you think that you can consistently act in your own best interest in trading?

In the book's second pillar, I provided a comprehensive framework for seamlessly integrating mindfulness into your daily routine through the S.T.A.Y. mnemonic. When we "stay" with our fears and discomforts, sitting with them and leaning into them instead of reflexively abhorring them, we embrace life in its entirety—the good, the bad, the ugly, the inexplicable. As a result, we find a sense of peace, and this allows us to lead more deliberate, meaningful, and fulfilling lives. We gradually open ourselves to the vast beauty and possibilities that both the market and life offer. To cater to the unique needs of traders, my team and I have developed specialized mindfulness practices tailored to the realities of trading. These meditations are available on my website and are designed to help you navigate markets with clarity, composure, and purpose. Feel free to explore these resources and make mindfulness a part of your daily routine.

That being said, mindfulness is unquestionably a vast and multifaceted subject. If my previous explanations thus far still haven't kindled a desire within you to establish a consistent practice, then the responsibility rests with me, as I may not have conveyed the topic in the most engaging and captivating manner. However, know this: your biggest competitors, the institutional players, are embracing mindfulness practices in unprecedented numbers. Prominent traders like Ray Dalio and Paul Tudor Jones have seamlessly integrated meditation into their daily routines. Ray Dalio went as far as saying, "*I have meditated for 48 years. It's been the biggest reason for my well-being and whatever success I've had*" (Dalio 2017). Trading firms that understand how the trading game is played are now urging their traders to adopt some form of introspective practice, which includes meditation. For instance, Goldman Sachs now offers their trading personnel meditation classes (Burton and Effinger 2014). These classes have gained such popularity that they're often fully booked with long waiting lists. The traction that mindfulness has gained in the financial sector is based on its proven effectiveness, not mere hearsay. A growing body of scientific research consistently demonstrates the positive effects of mindfulness meditation on brain function (Powell 2018). In the competitive landscape of financial markets, where even the slightest advantage can yield substantial results, finance professionals are actively exploring every possible edge. Mindfulness meditation is now recognized as a vital tool for mental sharpening in the high-stakes, high-pressure world of trading and investing. This paradigm shift toward mental and psychological conditioning reflects a broader acknowledgment that success in this fiercely competitive field extends beyond analytical and technical skills; it necessitates a trading composure. Hence, if you're not meditating, you're doing yourself a disservice.

The third quote, summarizing the key takeaways from the book's third pillar, is from Stephen R. Covey, an American author best known for his book *The 7 Habits of Highly Effective People*:

"Accountability breeds response-ability."

This insightful notion reminds us that accountability is about objectively assessing whether we've met our commitments without attaching additional judgment or emotional weight to the outcome. It's about asking simple, direct questions like *"Am I about to accomplish, or did I accomplish what I set out to do?"* This is where the role of a professional mentor or coach becomes incredibly valuable. Having accountability from someone with professional experience in trading offers much-needed guidance and structure amidst the vagaries of the market. Moreover, in a field where emotions often lead to significant setbacks, having a professional hold you accountable ensures that you remain grounded and focused on continuous learning and improvement. It's this blend of human insight, emotional support, and professional accountability that can transform the solitary pursuit of trading into a more structured and guided path to success.

In an ideal scenario, every trader would team up with an exceptional coach or mentor. If figures like Tudor Jones, with all their skill and success, recognize the value of external support and guidance, it highlights its indispensable role in achieving greatness. However, for many traders, financial constraints are often an issue. Additionally, the trading world is rife with individuals masquerading as experts, making it tough to identify genuine mentors. Despite these challenges, it's important to remember that self-accountability mechanisms exist to help you stay on course. While they may not be as impactful as the accountability provided by a professional, they can still act as effective stopgap measures. One practical method I've shared in Chapter 3 is the "Don't Break the Chain" technique. This tool is more than just a calendar; it's a visual commitment device that encourages consistency in any new habits you aim to establish, from meditation and exercise to diet and trading. By marking off each day you adhere to your plan, you create a chain of success that you'll be motivated to continue, reinforcing positive habits and discipline.

This "Don't Break the Chain" calendar cleverly taps into our innate loss aversion bias, a psychological principle that suggests we feel the pain of loss more acutely than the pleasure of gain. The fear of breaking a visually represented chain of successes leverages this bias to our advantage. Each consecutive mark on the calendar represents not just a day of adherence to our chosen habits but also an investment in our continuous streak of achievements. The longer the chain grows, the more we stand to "lose" if we break it, thus significantly amplifying our motivation to maintain our discipline. This visual and psychological reinforcement makes the calendar an exceptionally powerful tool for building and sustaining new habits, especially in fields as demanding as trading, where consistency and discipline are paramount. By transforming the abstract concept of consistency into something tangible, the calendar helps solidify our commitment to daily progress, making the abstract tangible and the intangible impactful.

There are other strategies you can employ to enhance your self-accountability in trading. Maintaining a detailed trading journal is another such strategy. Documenting your trades, including the rationale behind each decision and its outcome, allows for a retrospective analysis of your trading behavior. This introspection can reveal patterns, both positive and negative, guiding you toward strategies that work and away from repeated errors. Much has already been articulated about the critical role of journaling in trading, so I won't dwell excessively on that element here. The main point is that while the path to working with a competent trading coach may be fraught with obstacles, there are numerous self-accountability practices you can adopt to cultivate discipline, enhance your "response-ability," and navigate the market more effectively. These self-directed methods lay the groundwork for continuous improvement and can significantly impact your trading journey in case a personal mentor isn't currently an option.

To ensure accountability has a meaningful impact, it needs to be structured around key principles that ensure consistent progress and personal growth. In the book's fourth chapter, I present the A.C.T. framework, an approach designed to enhance accountability's effectiveness, whether or not you work with a coach or mentor. It encourages a proactive stance toward trading, where you're not only engaging the market but also actively engaging in self-improvement and strategic refinement. This way of approaching accountability is designed to empower traders to reach their full potential, making each decision a step toward greater success.

* * *

Combining the core principles of F.A.C.E., S.T.A.Y., and A.C.T., we forge a powerful guiding principle for our journeys into the realm of trading. F.A.C.E. teaches us the value of confronting uncertainty directly. By facing it head-on, we enhance our tolerance for the unknown, embracing the reality that the path through uncertainty is the only way forward. This direct engagement with uncertainty strengthens our resolve and equips us to navigate the chaotic waters of the market with confidence and resilience. S.T.A.Y. helps us integrate mindfulness into both our trading practices and daily lives. This principle encourages us to remain present with discomfort, to observe its transient nature, and to recognize that our fears and anxieties are often less daunting than they appear. By staying grounded in the present moment, we learn to observe market movements and our emotional responses without being overtaken by them, allowing for clearer, more composed decision-making. Finally, A.C.T. emphasizes the importance of advancing with accountability. It's about setting clear intentions, acknowledging our successes and areas for improvement, and committing to a journey of continuous learning and transparency in our actions. This proactive approach ensures that we not only react to the market with structure but also actively engage in a process of self-improvement and strategic refinement. Together, F.A.C.E., S.T.A.Y., and A.C.T. form a navigational triad, steering us through the vast ocean of trading with skill. This integrated approach makes trading profitable and enriches our personal journey, transforming trading into an expedition of profound growth and fulfillment.

Leveraging Your Strengths

Reflecting on my journey, I faced numerous obstacles in the market before achieving success. At its core, trading is a simple game; however, for psychological reasons, it can be incredibly challenging. Each of us has a unique tapestry of strengths and weaknesses. From the moment of our birth, our genetic blueprint sets the stage for our potential, influencing everything from our physical attributes to our mental predispositions. As we journey through childhood into adulthood, our environment, the challenges we face, and the lessons we learn further sculpt our mental and emotional landscapes. This conditioning is not merely superficial; it imprints upon us in profound ways, influencing how we perceive the world and react to situations. Hence, while mastering chart analysis and establishing trading rules comes relatively easily, creating behavioral consistency amidst uncertainty often proves to be a formidable task because our perceptions and reactions aren't always productive.

It is crucial to recognize that trading isn't a one-size-fits-all endeavor. Financial markets offer numerous paths to profitability; there are many ways to arrive at a positive expected value approach, statistically speaking. However, the multiplicity of these approaches, combined with our unique personal backgrounds, often leads traders to choose methods that match their wants but not their actual needs, from a personality point of view. Going back to my journey, it was marked by repeated setbacks, largely because I didn't understand my own nature. I was attracted to trading strategies that didn't fit my personality. In essence, I was desperately trying to fit a square peg into a round hole. Realizing this misalignment was a turning point in my journey. When I finally embraced a trading approach that espoused my personal characteristics, the change wasn't miraculous or instant—trading, with its inherent uncertainties, is challenging by nature. However, the alignment made the process somewhat smoother. No longer was I swimming against the current or fighting an uphill battle. There was a newfound harmony in my trading, allowing for a more natural flow in my decision-making, easing the daily grind and making a significant difference in my overall experience.

So, ask yourself the question: "Why not adopt an approach that leverages my strengths instead of spending my time fixing my weaknesses?" "What is a better use of my time?" There are no right or wrong answers to these questions, only what suits you best. Pursue what you find meaningful and fulfilling—just be clear about what that is. It's commendable to want to fix your weaknesses. Indeed, there are moments when addressing them is necessary. Yet, a pivotal and often overlooked strategy for personal growth involves the conscious decision to abandon pursuits that consistently elude our grasp in favor of those within our reach. Acknowledging that we cannot possibly excel at everything in every domain liberates us to focus our efforts where our greatest potential exists. What I'm emphasizing is that trading, at its core, aims to yield profits, ideally in a timely manner. Embracing a trading strategy that aligns with your strengths can streamline adherence to your trading plan, leading to a more consistent journey. For years, I struggled in my trading until I recognized this vital aspect. Adopting an approach that capitalizes on your strengths offers several benefits: (1) it alleviates emotional stress, (2) it simplifies adherence to your trading plan, and (3) it helps counteract psychological biases. When you combine such an approach with the principles outlined in this book, developing an embrace of uncertainty and the cultivation of composure, you set yourself on a path to becoming unstoppable in the market.

Understanding that trading is fundamentally a mental game allows us to appreciate the depth of our individuality. It invites us to explore not just who we are but why we are the way we are. This introspection can be empowering, offering insights into our core competencies and areas for growth. It encourages us to leverage our innate talents while acknowledging the areas where we might need support or development. By embracing our unique blend of strengths and weaknesses, we can tailor our trading approach and our entire financial strategy to better align with our authentic selves. You'll find a complimentary personality assessment tool for traders on the *Trading Composure* website. This tool, powered by AI, provides detailed insights into your trading personality and suggests the most suitable trading approach for you. Give it a try.

Closer Than You Think

Everyone, without exception, carries within them the capacity to become a consistent trader. This capacity represents the raw, unshaped potential that dwells deep within us, waiting to be honed, nurtured, and brought to the fore. Just as a block of marble holds within it a statue awaiting the sculptor's touch, each individual possesses the latent potential to master the intricate dance of trading. However, while capacity speaks of potential, ability is the realization of that potential. It's the manifestation of skill, whether innate or painstakingly acquired over time. While some individuals might have a natural inclination or a head start due to their inherent traits or early exposure, true mastery in trading often comes from disciplined practice, dedicated learning, and consistent effort. While everyone can dream of becoming a consistent trader, only those who channel their capacity through dedication, resilience, and continuous learning actually develop the ability to navigate the volatile waves of the market with grace and precision.

The challenge of trading lies not just in learning to read the market and developing a strategy but in the internal struggle, the battle against one's own instincts, fears, and biases. This introspective aspect of trading makes it a profoundly personal endeavor, where the greatest adversary and ally reside within oneself. It is in this internal arena where the real test unfolds, demanding not only technical knowledge and strategic acumen but also a deep

understanding of oneself. My aim in writing this book was to lay
out a comprehensive framework for cultivating what I call Trading
Composure, a state of mind that combines clarity, confidence, and
emotional equilibrium, essential for navigating the tumultuous
world of trading. This blueprint is designed not just to inform but to
transform, guiding traders through the intricate process of aligning
their mindset with the demands of successful trading. By integrating F.A.C.E., S.T.A.Y., and A.C.T. principles explored within these
pages, traders can expect to improve their market performance and
overall well-being. The ultimate goal is to empower traders to operate from a place of informed calm, where decisions are made based
on analysis and strategy rather than fear or greed.

As I mentioned at the outset, this book might not resonate with
everyone. Its core message, encouraging readers to accept and work
with uncertainty rather than attempting to eliminate it, challenges
the conventional wisdom of market prediction. This diverges from
the prevalent industry narrative that appeals to our deep-seated
desire for control over our financial destinies. Such a narrative has
shaped countless traders into believing they must become oracles of
the market, adept at calling every peak and trough. Consequently,
there's a tendency to gravitate toward those who display, or claim to
display, prophetic market insight. This often manifests in the form
of exaggerated success stories embellished with doctored results
and ostentatious symbols of wealth like luxury cars, mansions, and
private jets. Material success is seen as a hallmark of a "successful
trader," but it distracts from the real skills and mindset needed to
navigate the markets effectively. This book aims to shift that perspective, advocating for a more grounded approach to trading that
acknowledges the inherent uncertainty present in the market. It's
about developing the resilience and adaptability to respond to market movements with informed strategy rather than futile attempts
at prediction. Through this lens, success in trading becomes a matter of skillful navigation and risk management rather than the illusory promise of certainty and control.

In crafting this book, I steered clear of complex jargon. I'm just
a simple guy who, without the advantages of wealth or academic

accolades, has carved a successful path in the trading world. As I mentioned in the first chapter, my beginnings were humble. My name isn't accompanied by a long tail of titles such as PhD or MD. However, what I do have is decades of experience as a trader. I've also coached a significant number of traders, helping them achieve and sustain profitability in the market. My expertise doesn't lie in esoteric theories but in the practical, and the concepts and strategies I present in this book are ones I've personally implemented and have also been adopted by my students, resulting in remarkable progress and transformations. However, don't just take my word for it. Instead, I invite you to apply these principles in your own trading, observing and critically evaluating their efficacy. This book is designed to serve not as a prescriptive set of rules but as a catalyst for personal experimentation and discovery in the realm of trading psychology.

By sharing my journey and the lessons learned along the way, I aim to offer a relatable and accessible guide that empowers traders at all levels to explore their psychological landscape, challenge their limiting beliefs, and harness their inner strengths to navigate the markets with confidence and composure. This is a book about finding your own path to trading success, guided by insights born from genuine experience and a deep understanding of the psychological challenges traders face.

That being said, it's important not to just "get told" to develop your acceptance and appreciation of uncertainty and to nurture trading composure. Nobody learns by just getting told to do things. It's essential for you to engage in personal reflection on the nature of uncertainty and its implications for both your trading and life. You must actively piece together this understanding in your own mind, articulating your insights and emotions regarding this concept in your own words. This is where the practice of journaling can be helpful. Furthermore, merely understanding the concept of mindfulness on an intellectual level is insufficient. Many are well versed in the subject yet falter and lose their calm in challenging situations. Mindfulness isn't something to intellectualize; it is to be practiced. As for the aspect of accountability, securing a reliable accountability partner or manager is crucial. Choose someone capable of providing continuous, constructive feedback, aiding in your growth, and helping you stay on the consistency bandwagon. This can pay huge dividends.

Ultimately, it is not enough to only envision success. Dreams set the stage, but it's through deliberate action that dreams are transformed into reality. The success we achieve in the market is a reflection of our own development and character rather than just the outcome of our desires. Pursuing goals directly can often lead them to elude us, akin to chasing butterflies that just flutter away. Instead, by cultivating your own garden—focusing on personal growth and self-improvement—you create a space where butterflies naturally want to come, or in this case, success. We magnetize success by the essence of who we are, not by the sheer force of what we wish for. So, rather than "pursuing," focus on "becoming." My hope is that the insights shared in these pages have sparked a revelation within you, paving the way for a profound shift in your journey. You're closer to success than you think. Stay engaged with the market, manage your risk, remain insightful, and keep a positive attitude. Good things are on the horizon.

Acknowledgments

There are many people who directly and indirectly helped with this project.

First and foremost, I owe a great deal of gratitude to the late Dr. Van K. Tharp. I vividly recall a moment at a conference when he quietly shared with me that while my work might not be earth shattering, the power of my personal story and genuine approach would be its true value to others. He was right.

My heartfelt thanks go to several spiritual guides with whom I've had the privilege to study: Joseph Goldstein, Thich Nhat Hanh, Peter Levitt, and Michael Stone, just to name a few. On retreats, my inquisitive nature might have been overbearing. I am very grateful for their patience and guidance.

I am deeply thankful to the many students I've had the privilege of mentoring through the Consistent Trader Program. Your engagement and receptivity in discussing uncertainty and other topics have greatly helped me refine the ideas shared in this book.

A heartfelt Thank You to Shail Kotari for his expert management of the Consistent Trader Program during my focus on this project. As a consistent trader, former student of the program, and someone whom I consider a friend, there was no one better suited for the job than him.

My appreciation extends to my larger audience, who follow my work through newsletters and social media. Without them, there would be no Trading Composure.

I'm grateful to Bena for the interesting discussions we've had while I was writing this book. They helped in shaping some of the ideas presented here.

Finally, my deepest gratitude goes to my biggest cheerleader, Laetitia Jacquouton, who has been an unwavering source of support and sage advice throughout this journey.

References

"Anatta—Dhamma Wiki." https://www.dhammawiki.com/index.php/Anatta. *Wikipedia*, n.d. Accessed February 29, 2024.

Baer, Drake. "6 Reasons Wall Street Titans Love to Meditate." *Business Insider*, May 30, 2014. Accessed February 22, 2024. https://www.businessinsider.com/reasons-wall-street-titans-love-to-meditate-2014-5.

Burton, Katherine, and Anthony Effinger. "Serene Traders Make Killing as Wall Street Harnesses Meditation." *Bloomberg*, May 28, 2014. Accessed February 24, 2024. https://www.bloomberg.com/news/articles/2014-05-28/to-make-killing-on-wall-street-start-meditating?utm_source=nextdraft&utm_medium=email.

Dalio, Ray. *Twitter,* May 24 2017. Accessed February 29, 2024. https://twitter.com/RayDalio/status/867446044912742401.

Darvas, Nicolas. *How I Made $2 Million in the Stock Market: The Darvas System for Stock Market Profits.* Harriman House Limited, 2011.

De Palma, Brian, director. *Scarface.* Universal Pictures, 1983. 2hr., 50 min. https://www.netflix.com/title/60029681.

Douglas, Mark. *The Disciplined Trader: Developing Winning Attitudes.* Penguin Publishing Group, 1990.

Feloni, Richard. "Billionaire Investor Paul Tudor Jones Pays Tony Robbins Over $1 Million a Year and Emails Him Every Day—Here's What They Talk

About." *Business Insider*, November 2, 2017. Accessed February 24, 2024. https://www.businessinsider.com/tony-robbins-coach-paul-tudor-jones-2017-10.

Hanke, Stacey. "Three Steps to Overcoming Resistance." *Forbes*, August 14, 2018. Accessed February 22, 2024. https://www.forbes.com/sites/forbescoachescouncil/2018/08/14/three-steps-to-overcoming-resistance/?sh=4f2584905eae.

More, Maggie. "Winning the Mega Millions Jackpot Isn't Impossible, but It's Pretty Unlikely. Here Are Some More Likely Scenarios." *NBC Los Angeles*, July 29, 2022. Accessed February 24, 2024. https://www.nbclosangeles.com/news/local/winning-the-mega-millions-jackpot-isnt-impossible-but-its-pretty-unlikely-here-are-some-more-likely-scenarios/2951608/.

Nash, Jo. "The History of Meditation: Its Origins and Timeline." *PositivePsychology.com*, May 27, 2019. Accessed February 29, 2024. https://positivepsychology.com/history-of-meditation/.

Powell, Alvin. "When Science Meets Mindfulness: Researchers Study How It Seems to Change the Brain in Depressed Patients." *The Harvard Gazette*, April 9, 2018. Accessed February 29, 2024. https://news.harvard.edu/gazette/story/2018/04/harvard-researchers-study-how-mindfulness-may-change-the-brain-in-depressed-patients/.

Rolf. "Why Most Traders Lose Money—24 Surprising Statistics." *Tradeciety*, February 5, 2019. Accessed February 22, 2024. https://tradeciety.com/24-statistics-why-most-traders-lose-money.

Index